LIVING IN TWO WORLDS

Praise for *Living in Two Worlds*

Living in Two Worlds is a captivating memoir about a girl growing up in two different cultures, trying to figure out where she belongs. Vivian's ongoing quest to gain an understanding of her brilliant, beautiful, and complex mother is exquisitely written and lovingly told.
　—Sue Botelho

Rich in detail and compassionate in the telling, *Living in Two Worlds* is one woman's reflection on the dark secrets of childhood. Seeing the past through her parents' eyes, Pisano has written a love story to her family.
　—Nancy MacKay
　　Author of *Curating Oral Histories: From Interview to Archive.*

A grandfather's handsome study, a grandmother's sewing room, the scent of a mother's lipstick… a childhood suddenly interrupted…. Pisano reaches across international borders and across time, grappling with both simple and complex social circumstances, to treat the reader to a richly textured personal history, *Living in Two Worlds.*
　—Adrianne Aron
　　Author of *Human Rights and Wrongs*

LIVING IN TWO WORLDS

A Memoir

Vivian M. Pisano

Arc Light Books
Portland, Oregon

Living in Two Worlds: A Memoir

www.VivianMPisano.com/contact

ISBN: 978-1-939353-41-2
Library of Congress Control Number: 2021924587

Arc Light Books
Portland, Oregon

Para la familia Pisano

To be a woman is always to be hiding something.

—Sigrid Nunez, *A Feather on the Breath of God*

PREFACE

Memory is an odd thing: mysterious, unpredictable, unreliable. It is susceptible to errors. Facts and imagination merge. Fictitious events emerge as memories. She's not lying, others might say, she's just confused. "I'm not!" you may say. But can you be certain?

Much of my past is inaccessible; if not lost, then hidden, buried under the weight of time. Every so often a memory appears without warning, without my asking for it; it is just there, with a bang. I wake up in the middle of the night and see my mother's face, looking at me, full of love and longing. We'd had an argument. "You just don't know how I feel—you don't even care!" "Vivian, you don't know what a mother's love is, you've never had a daughter." My obstinacy sees only irritation on her face.

Or, like a shy violet peeking from behind its tiny dark green foliage, a wistful memory surfaces, quietly, into my awareness. With the mind still and open in those moments before full wakefulness I might sense a tart, sweet smell mixed with wood smoke. The warm sun reaches across my bedcovers and brings me a long-ago memory of my *abuelita* (my Chilean grandmother) outside, stirring a large cast iron pot of quince for the *membrillo* we loved to eat on our morning toast.

Memories surface without apology, without intent to threaten or delight. And they don't pretend to be of any vital significance. They just announce themselves and leave the why—if there is one—for us to figure out.

Other times, we pull and pull to dislodge a past experience or even just a single word. But no matter how much effort I exert, my stubborn brain just won't budge. I know that what I'm looking for is

1

somewhere in there deep down; it was there, once, but today, right now, I cannot get at it. That gate into my mind is closed. Maybe it'll open at some other time. Just let it be.

It has been a long time since I've had an early childhood memory, and of those, only a few survive. They appear as scant images, feelings, brief spaces in time that dug themselves out and, once exposed, remain there for me to ponder and wonder about their meaning. When did I dream those dreams of flying, of walking two inches above the ground? Why do I have an image of me burying my little plastic toy rabbit to hide it from others, but then, so successfully concealed, it was lost to me? It was pink, translucent, small enough to fit into my four-year-old hand, sitting upright, attentive, with its ears straight and tall. Secrets, buried and lost.

As time adds to the increasing weight of experience, the older memories sink deeper and are harder to dig out. The newer ones recede as well. Eventually even recent memories are obscured by layers of advancing life. More and more, toy rabbits lie lost somewhere in the mist.

Beauty and Promise

My mother's eyes were green—sparkling and full of life. Never clouding or fading, her eyes remained sharp and piercing throughout her seventy-six years. Celia, my mother, had a wide, prominent mouth, which she lipsticked flawlessly with one of the many Revlon colors she owned. She kept her favorite lipsticks on top of her dresser and the others at easy reach in the top drawer. I saw no logic in the arrangement of my mother's Revlons, unlike my crayons, which I kept in their original Crayola order. And her hunt for a particular tube of lipstick made more of a mess. In there somewhere was a color for every day, for every outfit. After some fumbling, my mother would pick up the matching tube, open the cap, and release the Revlon aroma of the crayon-like stick.

With steady hand, she'd roll it thickly onto full lips, then take a piece of toilet paper and blot once. Our bathroom's wastebasket always held her once-used, red-kissed tissue squares. Later, as her lips thinned, she re-created their fullness by painting lipstick just outside the edges. By my standards, I considered the look borderline gaudy. And it added a morsel of justification to add to a daughter's growing resentment of her mother.

My beautiful mother wore light makeup—powder, blush, no eyeliner, and no eye shadow. Until she reached middle age, when she drew on her once-perfectly arched eyebrows where they used to be, but with full and thick angular arches. She dabbed her eyelids with shadow, her eyelashes with mascara, and ran eyeliner around the perimeter of her penetrating eyes. Her waning eyesight prevented her from noticing the lack of precision in her application of makeup. I could see every imperfection.

My mother's nail polish—Revlon reds of all hues—matched her array of lipsticks. Her fingernails were oval-shaped, strong and smooth. I could never live up to those fingernails. Mine were shameful. I could not pull back my cuticles far enough to show half-moons. My fingernails broke and tore, they were so thin. Wistfully looking at her hands, I knew that it should be possible for me to have beautiful nails. It ran in the family. My older sister, Vicky, and younger brother, Jimmy, both had strong, shapely fingernails, and no hangnails. But those genes skipped me, the middle child. After a while, I threw away my manicure kit and just let my nails go. Let them do as they will. And I stayed away from nail polish, which might attract attention to them.

Such a pleasure to see those beautiful lipstick and nail polish hues mixed and matched and coordinated with my mother's finely constructed outfits! When she was forty-two and I was twelve, her mother, Grandma Stevens, my sister Vicky, and I had to throw away all her personal beauty products: doctor's orders. My mother was diagnosed with highly contagious tuberculosis. Although she had recovered from an earlier bout of TB as a young woman, it had resurfaced. Off she went to a TB sanatorium in the foothills fifty miles away from our home in Sacramento while her family filled wastebaskets with a full palette of Revlon reds.

My mother's toenails, however, were difficult—ingrown and thick and causing her much pain. I could've told her that those high heels she wore every day had brought on her foot problems. But high heels flattered her shapely legs and kept those nasty toenails out of view. My mother, a teacher, stood in them every day, all day long, in the classroom.

At her full height in bare feet, my mother stood five-foot-one. Small stature ran through my mother's female side of our family: grandmother, mother, aunt, sister, and I all hovered near five feet. Vicky was the shortest, at four-foot-eleven. Celia's was a well-proportioned body sustained by a diet-conscious routine. How could it be, then, that Vicky, the shortest of us all, filled size-D bra cups and I, at five-foot-two, could only get up to a B? Celia stayed with a middle C. But so many years of high heels distorted my mother's posture and threw her proportions off-balance.

Our mother had light, fine blond hair, cut above her shoulders in permed soft curls. Although I never saw it in its natural state, her hair was straight as a board, as Vicky often described her own hair, inherited from our mother. And never did I see that blond hair turn gray as she aged. Her hair, a Clairol-tinted blond, thinning with age, remained soft and fine. I resolved to never dye my hair, no matter how gray or white it became. Was that petty defiance?

Celia had skin so thin it looked transparent. I inherited that skin. One of the few memories I have of us that comes easily to me is of my mother and me standing in front of the bathroom mirror. She is behind me to the side, and I am fully facing my mirrored image. I complain about the noticeable blue veins branching across my chest. How unseemly they are! I look freakish. "That's a sign of beauty," the warm soft voice behind me says. How well she knows to comfort a seventeen-year-old girl, one who needs reassurance and affirmation about her looks. My school peers give me little fuel for self-confidence. I want to be attractive to them, accepted by them, like them. These visible veins, I feel, are a sign of thin skin, not of beauty. But I want to believe my mother, and so remain silent. I take in her words without protest.

Celia's high cheekbones, her nose not too big, not too small, just the right size for her round face. My abuelita, mother of my Chilean father, would tell me, "Look up there in the evening sky, at the full moon, just like your face." I could've added, "And like my mother's."

My mother came from a middle-class Midwestern family: a long American lineage of schoolteachers, farmers, ministers—people with modest occupations. She grew up in the 1930s and 1940s, the era when Hollywood filled movie screens with stories of affluence and glamour. Hollywood illusions took minds away from the reality of those harsh times leading up to and including the Second World War. Rita Hayworth, Bette Davis, Katharine Hepburn, Fred Astaire and Ginger Rogers; nightclubs filled with women in evening gowns and men in top hats and tuxedos. Women with cigarette holders in one hand and a highball in the other, accepting invitations to dance to the live swing music of big bands. Celia, like many young women of that time, became enchanted by the prospect of gliding through that world, wearing long, sparkling evening dresses and high heels, with blond curls brushing the tops of her shoulders. Imagination aside, Celia was serious about her education. Her goal, above all, was to become an educator, to share her love of learning with others. That was why she chose a prestigious university education.

Celia attended UC Berkeley in the late 1930s and early '40s, while the Second World War raged, and earned her master's degree with honors. Following graduation, she was ready to launch into a post as a professor, perhaps at a community college, a four-year college, or even, if lucky enough, a university. No. That was not the way for a recent graduate (and especially a female recent graduate) to start her educational career. Education opens some doors but leaves many closed. A job teaching at a high school opened, so she took it. Not much better than, in her opinion, the stenographer positions she had held during her college years.

While at college, Celia met someone. Not just anyone. Edmundo was a foreigner, from a far-away place, a Chilean exchange student pursuing a graduate degree in botany at UC Berkeley. Celia and Ed, as he was nicknamed in the US, met at an International House event. Ed was intelligent, fun-loving, and exotic. He wanted to marry her and take her back to Chile with him. Just as Celia had begun her teaching career and was discovering her penchant and aptitude for working with high schoolers, they married. They had a simple ceremony with no wedding costumes or attendants or party favors. Not even a lavish party, just a few family members and a handful of friends gathered at her mother's house to celebrate the couple.

Soon after their wedding, twenty-seven-year-old Celia and Ed, her twenty-six-year-old husband, whisked away to Ed's home country. And thus began her future daughter's list of unasked questions: What compelled my mother to give up a familiar and comfortable life in her own country, right at the start of a promising future? What could her new husband have said to her about life in a place most Americans did not know or much care about?

Here comes a man from a country whose language she studied in college, a country that would surely welcome the opportunity to hire highly educated American professionals to educate their children. After all, hadn't Americans been living comfortably in Chile since the early 1920s, when major US companies took control of Chile's valuable copper resources? Chile would provide Celia a chance to establish credentials and pursue a satisfying career there or in the United States, if and when she returned. She had no reason to look so far ahead.

On Shaky Ground

I was born in Santiago, the capital of Chile, my father's country. For ten years we lived in and around the capital and to the west, on the Pacific Coast. Although our little family moved from one rental house to the next, never staying long in any one place, I felt secure within our nest, with our large extended family always nearby.

"Earthquake! *Dios mío!*" Chileans yelled whenever the earth shook and houses rattled. They ran outside, into the streets. But my mother knew better. "Stay calm, stay away from windows, stand under the door frame," she would tell us. My mother was tough and resilient. Mere tremors didn't faze her. In my childhood country's shaky ground, we experienced frequent but minor quakes, and there never was a quiver too small to stop people from screaming and running outside. Tremors both thrilled and scared me; they felt like roller coaster rides. But I had never experienced a really big one. They had. Powerful earthquakes are common in Chile.

Chile runs along the west coast of South America. It is nearly as long as the United States is wide: 2,653 miles from the high desert plains in the north to the southernmost tip of the Chilean side of the island of Tierra del Fuego. At its broadest point, Chile measures only 221 miles from the Pacific Ocean to its eastern border with Argentina, high in the Andean cordillera. A mere forty miles traverse its narrowest point.

Active volcanoes in the Andes add drama to the landscape. The child in me would look at those tall white-capped mountains to the east looming over the capital city, Santiago—protectively sheltering us, or threatening malice? I wondered what running through snow felt like. Like bouncing on large wads of cotton? Did it taste like white cotton candy? Who could live like that up in the sky? They could easily fall off those craggy towers. Our teachers told us, "The Andes mountain range is the longest continental mountain range in the world. The only mountains taller than the Andes are the Himalayas." Although I never saw volcanic eruptions, I heard so many stories about the active Andean volcanoes that I sometimes pictured hot lava crawling down the mountain, eager to envelop us.

Since Chile stretches over so many latitudes, its landscape is bound to comprise extremes: The northern high desert plains claim to be the driest place on Earth, with moonlike topography. The fertile central valley, with its orchards, vineyards, and mild Mediterranean-like climate, reminded Celia of the Sacramento Valley, where she had lived since her teens. My early world was the central region of Chile, from Santiago to the fertile valley farmland of Limache and farther west to the beaches of Viña del Mar.

South of the central valley lies a complex fjord coastline and lush lake region. Farther down, the Andes cordillera ends with towers of spectacular peaks and glaciers in the Patagonia area. From there, a low moraine gives way to wide, windswept expanses. It is in this southern area where, years later, when my parents were no longer together, my father launched numerous expeditions and established expertise in the botanical life of the Patagonia.

Well-accustomed to California's own shaking ground, my mother found herself in familiar territory six thousand miles away from her home. Up until then, however, she had only experienced baby earthquakes. Although she arrived in Chile after the earthquake of 7.1-magnitude in 1945 that shook Santiago, she was 250 miles away from the epicenter during the stronger 7.9 quake the following year. Throughout her time in Chile, mid-'40s to late '50s, she felt many more; most of them were baby-type California earthquakes. I can guess that the tremors of this foreign land unleashed the homesickness she must have felt. And I wonder whether her homesickness unleashed tremors in her own body. A calm, stern exterior hid whatever turmoil may have lived internally.

Could Edmundo have fed Celia's illusions about his country before they married? After all, his father came from a prominent family and was the landowner of a large estate. But prominence is illusory, especially in a third world country. Many years later, my *tía* Sylvia, my father's sister-in-law, talked about the suitcase of fancy clothes my mother had sewn and brought with her to Chile—the evening dresses and up-to-the-latest-fashion suits. And spiky high heels she had purchased with her meager teacher's salary. She had filled a suitcase of expectations and illusions never realized.

Some may say she had expected to enter a higher-status society, where she could live with extravagance, wearing fancy clothes and furs. But I don't think so. Passion, love, yes. That's what I imagine. Hers was an infatuation so strong, it caused her to leave behind her accustomed and familiar way of life to accompany her new husband—a handsome, intelligent, yet-to-be-accomplished scientist—into a promising future. It's as if she were caught by the lure of love the shepherd speaks of in Christopher Marlowe's "The Passionate Shepherd to His Love:"

> *Come live with me and be my love,*
> *And we will all the pleasures prove*
> *That valleys, groves, hills, and fields,*
> *Woods, or steepy mountain yields.*

How could anyone resist such an allurement? Celia followed Edmundo "Ed" Pisano to make a home in Chile. There they lived for the next thirteen years: in Limache, in the resort town of Viña del Mar, in the port city of Valparaiso, and in the capital, Santiago.

Chile was not kind to my mother. She was conflicted. She loved her husband, her children, the amenities of a large, prosperous extended family, the beauty in such a serene and tumultuous land-scape. But the hardships were many to bear: the privations for our immediate family, the instability of my father's early career, cultural and social divisions that she could never fully break through, thwarted career aspirations, and illnesses. She couldn't have achieved the sense of belonging that she left behind, along with her mother, Grandma Stevens, in California.

Illnesses visited our family, and some stayed. For the most part, I was untouched by serious illness. Other than childhood diseases for which there were no inoculations at that time, I was healthy. Not so my older sister. Vicky was so weak at birth that she barely had enough strength to suck and could only be fed with a milk dropper. A diagnosis revealed that she had a heart lesion, a condition that would inevitably lead to a much-abbreviated life. At that time, no cure could save her and no corrective surgical procedure was yet available. Not until the mid-1950s, when open-heart surgery was developed, was there hope for a cure for Vicky's congenital heart condition.

My mother suffered her firstborn's condition, I imagine, from the powerlessness she felt, as a mother, to rid her child of her malady and improve her prognosis. I too suffered Vicky's weak heart, more so my conscience when my desire for a playmate trumped compassion for my sister. I wrestled with my conscience when I, the healthy child, was restrained from enjoying my very favorite activity, swimming, in solidarity with Vicky during times she was too sick to swim. "It's not fair!" I'd cry and stomp my foot. "Life is not fair," my mother would say. I was not so easily consoled, but acquiesced. Vicky and I would sit by the side of the pool watching our cousins jump and splash and shout in joy. Every once in a while, a spray of water would delightfully fall on me as I stepped in front of my sick sister to shield her. Only much later in life did I realize that my mother was teaching me empathy.

Celia's health also suffered, especially during her first few years in Chile. A foreigner, she could not escape illnesses that afflict those who enter an environment for which they have yet to build immunities. Tía Sylvia told me that while my mother was pregnant with me, "the poor woman began to have lots of health problems." Appendicitis during the pregnancy was followed by surgery after my birth. Then came other complications. Both she and my father fell ill with typhoid fever. Left in a weakened state, my mother contracted bronchopneumonia. While she was in the hospital for that latest affliction, the doctors discovered hepatitis and tuberculosis in her young, compromised body.

Her afflictions pulled us apart physically and then emotionally. With the TB diagnosis, my mother was admitted to a sanatorium for a yearlong sojourn. My abuelita took me in, a baby only six months old. Relatives told me she cuddled and coddled and gave me all that my mother's child-rearing books warned against. I was spoiled. Not by my mother but by my abuelita. I developed an attachment to Abuelita that grew in strength during that baby year and weakened ties to my own mother.

During the year as my surrogate mother, Abuelita took the opportunity to have me baptized. She knew my mother would undertake no such Catholic ritual. But Abuelita could not let her beloved granddaughter remain in the state of original sin. It was her duty as a devout Catholic to ensure my deliverance from this unholy state. She scheduled my baptism to take place along with my cousin Juan's. Abuelita brought us up to the altar, a swaddled child in each arm. The priest sprinkled water on our heads and named us, Juan and Vivian. Only after the ceremonial words were uttered did anyone realize I had been named Juan and my cousin, Vivian.

When I was five, another sister arrived. Valerie's was a short life. Born healthy, our baby sister was seven months old when before going to bed one night, my mother found Valerie unresponsive in her crib. My parents rushed her to the hospital, but SIDS (sudden infant death syndrome) had already taken her life. That night my mother woke my sister and me before dawn and told us that Valerie's death was caused by a ruptured vein. That night we cried, the three of us together, hugging, until, exhausted, I fell back to sleep.

Two years later, Jimmy arrived. I was seven and Vicky nine, much too old to be his playmates but appropriately old enough to pamper him and taunt him. Had she lived, Valerie would have been his ally. For my mother, Jim was a miracle after the death of her infant daughter. With this baby, my parents dropped their established naming convention for the V girls: James was named to honor my mother's father, whom she had lost as a teenager.

My sister and I had to help our mother with our brother's care. Oh, the diapers! We changed them, cleaned them, washed and folded them.

A year after he was born, I had my tonsils removed. As I lay on the operating table, the doctors placed a white, damp cloth on my face and told me to count to ten. Just a few numbers, and the next thing I knew, I awoke with a soreness in my throat, asking for the ice cream I'd been promised to soothe my throat.

"How did it go?" my mother asked.

"The last thing I remember is the smell of that wet cloth, just like Jimmy's diapers."

Fundo de la Gloria

We spent our summers on my grandparents' estate, Fundo de la Gloria, an agricultural farm, a ranch, and a vineyard in the country, near the small town of Limache in the central part of Chile, about one hundred miles west of Santiago toward the coast.

My grandfather Don Edmundo was the *patrón* of the estate, but to us he was Nono, a vestige of his Italian roots. He was a towering giant in stature, command, and largesse—to the fundo's many workers, to family members, and to visitors. His study held the sensations of a man's study: deep earthy smells, traditional leather seats, sheepskin rugs and throws, dark paintings, deeply hued darkening drapes, leather-bound books on all the shelves, a large imposing wooden desk.

I picture him entering his room and opening the heavy wooden door in one authoritative, confident movement. A heavy wool poncho covers his torso; gray streaks fleck his hair and moustache, his face sun-tanned and wrinkling from the dry summer sun. The air is crisp in here, kept dark so that it remains cool throughout the hot summer day. This is his room, his office. Paperwork awaits him. In the prime of his life at fifty years old, he'd rather be outside on his Chilean fleece-and-leather working saddle cinched to his favorite horse, riding over his land, tending to the work to be done. This man's work is never done. Especially when the work is a farm.

Nono and Abuelita's farmhouse was large enough for our entire family to stay during the summers—three months with all the cousins swimming, horseback riding, playing childhood games, and delighting in the special love that our abuelita had for all of us.

Abuelita embodied the typical Chilean woman's role: mistress of the household and, in her case, in charge of a group of maids: housecleaners, kitchen assistants, and gardeners. She supervised the kitchen and house help and joined them in their work. Abuelita was the meal planner, organizer, and, to our delight, cook. She was the chef; anyone else involved in meal preparations could only be a sous-chef. On our summer vacations at the fundo she'd be sure to make her grandchildren's favorite treats: *humitas, choclo,* sopaipillas, *torta de mil hojas.* This was my comfort food.

Managing a houseful of adults and children could not have been easy. Mornings for her were taken up with kitchen tasks. We children stayed out of her way and took our playful mischief outside until the call for lunch. After our main midday meal, time slowed down. Abuelita would spend many afternoons in the sewing room—a small, slightly elevated room on the first floor overlooking the front garden. Its high, large bay windows were framed with light, gauzy curtains and window seating. I loved to spend lazy afternoons in the sewing room, especially when it was raining outside. I read on the soft pastel-colored pillows while embraced by my grandmother's presence. She attended to her embroidery, picking among an array of silken embroidery threads of all colors—more colors, even, than in my largest Crayola sets. We'd sit in the sewing room, I on the window seat with my book, she in her cushioned wicker chair, embroidering or darning, comforted by the silence of our tasks, reassured by each other's presence.

Their house was set back from the main north-south road. In those times, the early 1950s, traffic was sparse. Few vehicles drove on the main thoroughfares. And at night, only occasional trucks delivering goods from and to the farms and towns could be heard. I would lie in my bed and let the far-off sound of traveling trucks lull me to sleep.

The house had two stories and two entrances. The formal entrance was for guests, on the left end through a small front garden; the main entrance, the one used by the family, was on the right corner. This door opened to a short hallway with the sitting room that was also used for sewing on the left, and a small bedroom on the right. In that room Vicky and I were put down for naps on twin beds. During one nap time, when we were quite young—Vicky five and I three—she rolled a small piece of newspaper, put one end to her mouth, struck a match, and lit the other end. She was going to smoke, like all the adults did. But this was no cigarette; the newspaper flared. She threw the burning paper down on the bed. I woke to a room full of smoke and flames, my sister screaming, adults rushing in and carrying us to safety.

The house did not burn down. Everything was quickly doused with water, leaving the room smoke-damaged but no worse. Bedcovers and curtains were singed. No one was hurt. No boxes of matches were ever again left behind in that room. Still, Vicky refused to take her naps there any longer.

From inside the house, we children liked to run toward the family entrance and stop short of the sliding glass door at the end that gave way to a patio, with a view of the back garden and the landscape beyond. We played a hopscotch type of game on the tree stump pavers embedded in the hall floor along the sliding glass door. And we were short enough to jump on the pavers all the way across the hall's end, underneath an open-step stairway. There we'd reach up to hang on the steps and swing back and forth.

The stairway led to upstairs bedrooms. The landing at the top of the stairs reminded me of a landing that one would find in a hotel, with a few pieces of furniture—chairs, tables, lamps. All around the landing were bedrooms, maybe five or so. The two I usually stayed in were either the one on the left, with a small balcony that looked toward the road, or the room down the hall from the landing. I liked the second room the best; it had a bathroom right next to it. This bedroom and bathroom looked over the front part of the house toward the barns and winery and workers' living area. We could climb out of the bedroom window and walk on the gently sloping roof to reach the bathroom window.

Our grandparents' room was set at an angle on the corner of the second floor. It had a small balcony and multiple windows overlooking the entrance of the property. On some mornings Nono and Abuelita would invite me to their bed to snuggle with them. Oh how the warmth of their bodies and the rising sun comforted me!

The living room (called simply "living") was downstairs on the opposite side of the house next to the formal front entrance. Not a room for children, other than for special events. Christmas, occurring in the middle of summer, was celebrated there. The empty fireplace was used for the crèche. A locally cut pine tree soaring to the ceiling and decorated with glass balls and homemade tinsel was our tree. Underneath were presents for the children—probably for adults too, but those gifts were not our concern. A party was held before the midnight dinner for adults. That was when we children went to bed.

Summertime at the Fundo de la Gloria was, for us cousins, the highlight of our year. There we learned how to ride horses, swim, crush grapes with our bare feet, find the ripest berries among brambles, and lose ourselves in the many hidden paths. The fundo seemed to have no boundaries to a small child. And every year we were there, I discovered a new place, a new hidden treasure.

From the house was a short path to the swimming pool. The first part of the path passed next to a corral, where rams and a few sheep were kept. Although they were behind barbed wire, they still frightened me when the horny male sheep ran menacingly up next to me as I walked by. How could I be a threat to their masculinity? As the path neared the pool area, it became a grapevine-laced arbor that led to a large brick gazebo-like area with a large parilla— an outdoor brick oven. This was where summer parties were held. Beyond was the pool with changing rooms at opposite ends, one for men, the other for women.

Except for breakfast, mealtimes at the fundo were times for the family to gather together. Breakfast was a simple, scant meal meant only to break the long night's fast: toast with marmalade, toast with avocado, and coffee or tea. On special mornings, the maid would enter our room with a breakfast tray that we'd place on our laps for a breakfast in bed.

Lunch, the main meal of the day, was served around two in the afternoon. We were served in courses: soup, entrée (only on special occasions), main dish, dessert, then either *cafecito* or *tecito* or *aguita*. A cafecito was an espresso-like coffee, served in a small cup. After meals were the only times "real" coffee was consumed: coffee at breakfast or teatime was mostly powdered Nescafé. An aguita was an herbal tea, lemon verbena (*cedrón*). At the fundo, lunch was served in the dining room, on a large oval table, a room adjacent to but separate from the "living."

Children were fed a snack between the meager breakfast and late lunch. Typically our 11:00 a.m. snack was a cottage cheese–like foodstuff, Chilean *quesillo*, held together in one gelatinous mold. It made me gag. When I later went to the United States, cottage cheese reminded me of quesillo. I never did learn to like it.

As small children, we often ate lunch and dinner in the kitchen, where we didn't have to practice our table manners. We were freer to play with our food, making words out of our alphabet soup, and hide inedible food in our napkins. But the maids kept us in line, made sure we behaved and ate well. At 5:00 p.m. the family would all gather in the dining room for tea, coffee, and, as with breakfast, toast and marmalade, toast and avocado, and tortes and biscuits.

Abuelita had the sad eyes that she gave *Papo,* my own made-up derivative of *Papá* that I used for my father. Pale blue eyes that cried when she was happy. She cried when she welcomed us, as if she had spent all the time since we were last with her missing us. Abuelita was always busy, using her hands to embroider, stitch, stir, beat egg whites to triple their size and drop by dollops on the sweet curd before placing the dish in the oven. I'd find her peeling, dicing, succumbing to tears from the white onions she diced so adeptly.

Our family all loved Abuelita. She never showed an angry or strained face or used a shrill, angry voice. She offered only a calm and soothing demeanor. If she had another side, I never saw or heard of it. "She may be simple," my father told me, "but she is loving and kind and generous." I had never even thought of assigning an intellectual label to her. It had never occurred to me. It was irrelevant.

I treasured spending my childhood summers in such an idyllic country setting. The fundo's house was my sanctuary, the surrounding land my playground. I felt such great joy riding on the tamest mare down the dusty road toward the vineyards, then trotting out the road past the vineyards and almond orchards with their trees full of light pink flowers, falling like soft, thick snowflakes. Riding away from the house, the fastest I could get that horse to go was a bouncing trot. Only when we turned around to go back would she finally gallop, while I sailed above.

Love Endures

A wedding picture of my parents hung on Grandma Stevens' wall: Celia, a Marilyn Monroe-like beauty, with curled blond hair, wearing a typical '40s woman's suit, the snug jacket following the trim contours of her shapely figure. No white-lace gown and veiled crown for her. She holds a large bouquet of white flowers and gives the camera a wide, self-assured, confident smile. Ed is serene, relaxed, and serious despite his lighter, carefree side. Ed, like Celia, had been a serious student, yet unlike her, he was also a daredevil and a jokester. His feathered eyebrows, which would grow into dragonfly-like wings in his older years, are evident even then.

The picture is lost; it exists only in my memory. Its palette of black-white-gray was typical of photographs in the '40s. Simple shades allow the softness and creaminess of the skin to come through, conveying the couple's vulnerability and innocence. There, too, are the sharp angles of brusqueness and decisiveness. Most of all, my mind's eye sees an imagined future of hope and love. When did all these features blend together and form a complex, troubled, self-reliant, determined, veiled woman? A woman who would give me the tough love she had received from her mother.

Although he had been working as an agronomy engineer while in the United States, as well as earning a few dollars painting houses in his spare time, my father couldn't have had many financial resources for travel. Grandma Stevens, Celia's mother, contributed some, and surely Ed's father—Nono—contributed more to bring his eldest son home with his new wife.

Theirs would have been a long honeymoon if they had cruised down the Pacific Ocean. I believe they chose the shorter route by air. They were not people with leisure time to spare or the resources to revel in luxury. My parents, as I knew them, leaned toward the side of practicality. My romantic imagination, however, prefers to see them spending two weeks or more traveling the Pacific Ocean, southward by ship.

But I'm sure they felt a cautious jubilation with the war ending, and an unrestrained jubilation of starting a new life wrapped in each other's love. Their first child, Vicky, was already fluttering in Celia's belly when they arrived in Chile.

The young couple looked forward to Ed embarking on a career in his native country. But it was wartime, and nothing was certain. In 1944—the year before—Chile had entered the war with the Allies. Subsequently, although the country remained politically stable, the scarcity that followed fomented high inflation and social turmoil.

The Chile that my mother came to in 1945 resembled little of the first world country she had left behind. Chile was just emerging from the Great Depression of the 1930s, which had severely affected Chile's economy; the League of Nations had declared Chile the country hardest hit by the Depression. Chile's economy was and remains centered on the rich copper mining yield of the Atacama Desert in the north of the country. Chile depended on its mining exports, and global demand for these minerals waned during those years. Chile was a third world, referred to then as "undeveloped," country.

Daily life had offered none of the conveniences to which Celia was accustomed. Although Ed came from a prosperous family, prosperity, in the Chile of that time, was no offset to the realities of the country's struggle. Neither the generosity of in-laws nor the skills of a well-educated husband could place my mother in the middle-class comfort she had known in the States. My father could barely support his family with his earnings as a university professor.

In another photograph: joy in the eyes of my young mother, newly arrived in Chile, posing with three other women—two of my aunts and a friend. All look straight at the camera, happy, poised, and relaxed. They dress in conventional suits—modest straight skirts and fitted jackets buttoned over fancy, light-colored delicate blouses. How I wish it were not just a black-and-white photo—so lovely to have seen what colors each of those women had chosen for her blouse! But the nature of black-and-white invites a deeper look. Something else shines through my mother's countenance: expectation, adventure, confidence; the picture of someone who loves and is loved.

In this land of geographical extremes, my mother found her own life defined by extremes: on one side, passionate love for her new husband and expectations for a charmed life among a well-to-do family; on the other, disillusionment over the hardships she encountered, the illnesses and separations ahead of her.

Tía Sylvia told me years later, "They both loved each other so much. Your *mami* arrived in Chile with such hopes for the future, looking ahead to a prosperous and comfortable life. She brought a suitcase full of beautiful evening dresses for parties that seldom occurred. Illnesses she contracted here and the pain she felt for the poor health that befell her children . . . and your parents' financial difficulties. No wonder your mami became disillusioned with Chile."

Disillusionment. I believe it placed a shell around my mother. She was a woman who was driven by a resolute will and expressed her love with a firm hand. "Spare the rod, spoil the child" was not her motto. "Don't pick up a crying baby and comfort her with your hugs and kisses. She needs to learn to sleep when it's time to sleep." Strict discipline, my mother earnestly believed, prepared the child for life ahead. My mother's favorite proverb, "If wishes were horses, beggars would ride," was her answer to my pouty "Why can't I?" questions. Apparently, none of my Chilean aunts followed her child-rearing principles. They followed their maternal instincts. I wanted to be spoiled too.

The firm-hand approach persisted throughout Celia's mothering. She even counseled her own daughter to follow this strategy: "No, Vicky, don't go into your daughter's room to pick her up and console her. You'll just spoil her. Let her stay in her room and cry it out. Then she'll go right to sleep."

Drama surrounded the couple that was my parents: explosive arguments, never physical or abusive, but loud, yes. Yet their arguments were short. And, she told me, "they ended in sweet love." Theirs was a passionate, at times volatile, relationship, with flaring tempers.

"Jesus Christ!"
"Dammit, Ed! I told you before."
"Celia, I don't have the money!"
"But we need it, and we can afford it. It's not trivial."

I often didn't understand what their arguments were about. I didn't even try. I just wanted to stay in my own world, shut out the noise from the bedroom down the hall, and play with my dolls. After the eruptions, I knew that if I waited just a bit longer, silence would come along and calm the atmosphere. My dolls agreed, and then it was time to put them to bed.

At the time my mother arrived in Chile, the United States had 133.5 million inhabitants, and 9.5 million of them lived in my mother's home state of California. Chile was a country with a population of a mere 6 million. The majority of the population comprised a mixture of Indigenous and European descendants. African heritage was almost nonexistent. I never encountered any Black Chileans during my ten years there.

Chile prided itself on its lack of racism, but racism shows through its class system: the higher the class, the lighter the skin, and the lower, the darker. I never met a maid, farmworker, or laborer without the darker shading of Chile's Indigenous people. Wealth did not play the major role in this class system. Within my family, skin color spanned the light-to-dark spectrum, and those with coloring on the darker side were teased: *"Negrito,"* I heard aunts and uncles call my olive-skinned cousins, as a term of endearment with a splash of condescension.

My father's family reflected the majority mix, although with a strong representation of white European ancestry. The patriarchal line came from Italy, but there were also some antecedent lines from English and German settlers during the nineteenth and twentieth centuries, and some from other South American countries as well. Our family, like so many families throughout the world, has a history of migration experiences, and so, like other families, mine is a mixture of ethnicities.

The Pisanos are, as Chilean families tend to be, tightly knit. Loyalty and support come first, no matter how errant any one individual member might be. The individual who strays from the norm is shielded from outside scrutiny and anticipated scandal;

the deviation is kept private, not discussed. We pretend it doesn't exist. I never heard anyone in my strongly Catholic family mention my father's disbelief in God. As his daughter, I wouldn't know if they did have mournful or disapproving conversations among themselves about his fall from grace. Any such talk would have taken place only after he and we, as his immediate family, were out of hearing range. But were that conversation to come up in a gathering with people outside the extended family, any one of our relations present would stand up in protest of such remarks. Protect the relative. Keep family affairs private. That comes first.

As a child, I was unaware of such social behaviors. Only years later, when I returned to Chile as an adult, did I realize that convention discourages face-to-face criticism. But once the target of criticism has left the room, commentary restrictions are lifted. "Yes, *viejita*," I heard my father say to an elderly family relation as he accompanied her to the door, "you are always welcome here, and we enjoy your visits and conversation." Once she was out the door and out of earshot, my father rejoined our company, and all mocked her gently. "She runs off at the mouth," "Talk-talk-talking all the time," "She just can*not* stop talking," "I can't remember anything she said, she talked so much!" But this was not a conversation to be had outside our family network. Our elderly relation could be assured that none of us would betray her in "mixed" company.

Chilean family members of all ages outnumber friends at parties and celebrations. At every family gathering I've been to while I lived in Chile and then in my return trips there, kissing every person on the cheek upon arrival and again at departure is routine. I wonder what my mother thought about this custom; she was never one to demonstratively show affection—not to me, not to strangers. But this is the family that welcomed Edmundo's *gringa* wife upon the couple's arrival.

Celia's Protestant background seemed out of place in Chile. Catholicism was the country's dominant religion, and although church and state had been constitutionally separate since the 1920s, Roman Catholic rituals and celebrations permeated social and official events. Within the family, the women all followed the Roman Catholic faith, the men marginally so, and my father not at all; he was an atheist.

There was little churchgoing in my immediate family. Occasionally my mother would take my sister and me to a Protestant church. But we always celebrated the traditional Christian holidays of Easter and Christmas. For Americans and other people from the Northern Hemisphere who associated Easter with spring and Christmas with midwinter, celebrating these holidays in their opposing seasons was disorienting. And it was baffling to see winter scene decorations and Santa Claus in his red snow suit driving his reindeer-pulled sled all the way from the North Pole to the Southern Hemisphere's midsummer Christmas. Easter came in autumn, causing egg hunts to move indoors during inclement weather.

My summers in Abuelita's house included attending Catholic Church services every Sunday. They were conducted in Latin, so I understood not a word. But what entered my awareness were the resonating rhythmic sounds of the priest's sermon and the echoing voices of the choir with one high soprano sound reaching up and soaring above the rest. Although I understood nothing nor learned anything from going to church, a sense of the mysterious embedded itself deep within me.

My mother studied Spanish in college, although what she learned was the clearly enunciated Mexican Spanish. Her immersion in Chilean Spanish—a fast-talking consonant-swallowing dialect— left her flummoxed. This Spanish was a different foreign language to her. There were, fortunately, a few English-speaking family members, but everyday conversations in English were rare.

Later, when I came along, I never became used to her way of pronouncing the language that was native to me. She spoke gringo Spanish. Hearing her unapologetically mangle the sounds embarrassed me. Hence in our household, I spoke Spanish with my father and sister, and English with my mother.

So too was she out of sync with the local way of dressing. My mother found upon arriving that Chilean women's approach to fashion differed from hers. Clothing, according to Chilean standards, masked the body rather than emphasizing or revealing the contours of its hills and valleys. Fashionable suits were constructed from subdued, dark colors and worn with a frilled but more often a simple white blouse. Summer printed dresses were buttoned to the neckline. My mother preferred a touch of provocation in her dress, whether it was a bold color, a sensuously tactile fabric, a modern design not yet seen in Chile, or a teasing neckline. On hot summer days I was ashamed by the shorts my mother wore, hoping no visitors would come by. Wasn't she aware what was proper attire?

A New Life for Celia

Upon arriving in Chile, my parents lived with Edmundo's parents in their Fundo de La Gloria, in the central region of the country. My mother was determined to adapt, to fit into the new culture, while maintaining her American ways.

Never having traveled out of the country, with only college Spanish, my mother abandoned her accustomed California life for the completely foreign environment that was Chile. Chile was so unlike anything she knew. Government services were meager; public health suffered. There were few household conveniences. Electricity and utilities had to be conserved; the frequent brown-outs prevented indulgence. My own habit of turning off the light as I exit a room comes from my father's lessons so ingrained in him during that time. Prosperity in my father's large family was not a given and held no future guarantee. Chile was a poor country.

What turbulence must have swirled in my mother's mind! Torn between love for her husband and mourning the loss of her accustomed world; lured by the possibilities of a glamorous, exotic life and facing shattered expectations; pulled by the intrigue of living in a new culture, yet pushed down by its difficulties. My mother found herself between a familiar life, now abandoned, and a new life, for which she was unprepared.

I want to go home. I don't belong here. I can't speak their language. Daily tasks are too time-consuming, too demanding. These are words

I imagine having traveled through her mind. They are words that would travel through my own mind over a decade later.

But hers was a stalwart nature. She inherited the Protestant ethic whereby work is expected to be hard; you make the best of what you've been given and continue on.

Abuelita took on teaching her daughter-in-law the Chilean way. My mother's college Spanish was forced into life, since Abuelita spoke no English. Years later, on my first trip back to Chile after I had left for the US, Abuelita's eagerness to impress me with the few English words she had learned touched me. "Lunch" was one of those words she knew (she pronounced it more like "launch"). She used that word at every opportunity, regardless of whether it was time for breakfast, tea, dinner, or even lunch. And, as Chileans are wont to do, she made diminutives of that word: *lonchito* and even *lonchitito.*

Knowing Chilean Spanish idiosyncrasies and idioms, greeting traditions, social customs, family lore, and how to prepare typical Chilean dishes are among the tools necessary for an immigrant, and much more for the American wife of a member of an entrenched Chilean family. My mother absorbed these lessons as she worked and lived alongside her mother-in-law in those early months of her new life.

I can picture my abuelita telling my mother, "We start the day early with a light breakfast. Mornings are for shopping and preparing the midday main meal, which is served at 2:00 pm. Afternoons are for napping, sewing, gardening, or an afternoon stroll until teatime (called *once,* pronounced "awn-say" in Chilean Spanish) at 5:00 p.m. Tea and coffee, toast and jam and cheese, are served at this time, or even a more substantive meal. Or, the *once* can be the occasion for a party, with little cakes and Chilean *dulces* as well as savory dishes. A light meal is served for dinner late in the evening." My mother, being the independent woman I knew her to be, followed her mother-in-law's advice selectively. After she and my father moved to their own home, they reverted to the American mealtime schedule.

"Two women cannot run the same household," one of my aunts allegedly said of my mother's living with her in-laws. A mild tension between the two women was born. I sensed this unease as a child while I was shielded from it. Abuelita and my mother—two women of different ages, diverse cultures, in love with the same man: one as mother, the other as wife.

Cultural, and perhaps personal, differences strained their relationship. Abuelita was fearful and superstitious, my mother fearless and rational. As for me, starting from a very early age, I intermingled fantasy and fear. Fear of the dark—not fear of a plausible or tangible threat, but fear of imaginary, terrifying nonhuman creatures—plagued me throughout and beyond my childhood. My mother, I later learned, attributed that fear to my abuelita's influence. How could her fears not enter the psyche of a young, vulnerable child with whom she was so close?

I sensed that part of Abuelita's motivation to indoctrinate my mother in Chilean ways came from her and Nono's hope that their eldest son, Edmundo, would eventually take over Fundo de La Gloria. Not only was their fundo a working estate, but also it was the family go-to place for summer vacations and family gatherings. Abuelita understood her role to prepare their son's wife for the job she would cede to my mother.

Other family members did not accept such a plan so easily. They had, I believe, an underlying reluctance to have a foreigner, an American woman, take over our beloved family matriarch's role. My mother neither wanted nor was destined for that role. She may have enjoyed the status of a farm owner's wife but not its duties.

If my father had ever entertained taking over the running of the fundo, he no longer held such intentions. His aspirations lay in scientific research, rather than in the daily running of a farm. And so he launched a career in botany that eventually grew into great prominence and distinction but brought little income, especially in those early years.

My parents found a little house to rent in the town of Limache, about ten miles from the family farm. It was a spare house with no heat, other than from a fireplace, and a wood stove for cooking. It had no washer or dryer, no machines to substitute for physical work. After my parents were well settled in their own home, my mother sought household help. She hired a live-in maid to help her with household chores, as did most middle-class Chilean families. But planning and cooking the meals—at first with her own American recipes—were her domain. Not until she settled into the country did she embrace the local cuisine. She sewed her clothes and ours, as many Chilean mothers did, but used only American patterns. She socialized, both with my father's family and with the English-speaking community, American and British.

Early in her inauguration to this unfamiliar country, my mother planned to cook a chicken for dinner. She asked the maid to pick one up while shopping that afternoon. She did, and what came home with the maid was a very live and active chicken. At that time, a Chilean market chicken clucked all the way home. American cooking chickens are lifeless, drained and plucked, oven-ready. I picture my mother's face drained of her warm blood, that first time she contemplated the task ahead—a task she had to learn how to do and a task that required her to learn how to transcend her innate revulsion to slaughter and its mess. I think of the expression so in vogue in the twenty-first century, "farm to table." In the Chile of the 1940s and early 1950s, we had no such expression but lived its meaning. This was one of many lessons that my mother had to master about her new life.

As a child, I didn't wield any axe, but I saw poultry heads being chopped and headless birds hanging upside down with a pot below to catch their draining blood. A chicken or two and occasionally a duck hung motionless in the backyard, being prepared for our Sunday dinner. I would sit and watch with fascination as the dark red viscous liquid dripped down into the metal bucket until the last drop. Once the chickens were ready for the kitchen, I helped with the feather plucking. I did not like that job. It was smelly, messy, slow. The naked, plucked chicken is not pretty. It looks emaciated, full of goose bumps. For us children—my sister and our cousins— our favorite part was pulling the tendons of the severed chicken feet this way and that to open and close the claws in playful ways. I grew up in this Chilean world, whereas my American mother, used to buying packaged poultry at Raley's supermarket, was confronted with a new reality all at once.

Although we were among those with meager means, not only did we have a live-in maid, but also another who came once a week for washing and ironing, and another for house cleaning. I loved to be home on those Saturday afternoons with the young maid who came to clean. As soon as my parents left the house, she turned up the radio full blast and sang along with the latest popular music. The emerging rock-and-roll tunes of the 1950s were alluring and contagious; I soon learned to sing out David Seville's "The Witch Doctor" ("Oo ee oo ah ah ting tang walla walla bing bang"), the Coasters' "Yakety Yak," and Little Richard's "Tutti Frutti." With a broom as her dance partner, our maid swept the floors while Vicky and I, unable to contain ourselves, joined in the fun.

Having come from a small family with no close relations beyond Lola, a paternal aunt who lived in Savannah, my mother was unprepared for her husband's large and insular family. As a group they were loyal regardless of opposing social, political, or religious inclinations. In Chile, members of the immediate family mingle daily with members of the extended family. You are never out of reach of family; you are never alone. Even after many years and from afar, I would feel the pull of my Chilean family. And with every visit, they'd bring me into their bosom, no matter how much time had gone by. "Why," my cousin Sylvita asked me, "do you say you feel you're imposing on us? You're family. It's simple: we love you; you are part of us."

When my mother first started her teaching career, she aspired to teach college-age students, students who had chosen to pursue knowledge rather than those for whom school was mandatory. But for a woman at that time, particularly a woman starting her career and a marriage, an academic faculty appointment was hard to come by. Better to start in a primary or, as she did, secondary school.

Marriage and emigration cut short her career path just after it began. She left her teaching assignment—as recorded in her curriculum vitae—"to reside in South America." Such a short, curt statement for a life-changing event!

Determined to pursue her work, my mother resumed teaching in a Santiago secondary school shortly after my sister's birth. She taught in the same British school that I would eventually attend. However, once again her teaching stint was cut short, this time by her pregnancy with me.

Celia dove into homemaking, honing her cooking and sewing skills. We, her children, were spoiled not by her motherliness but by her delectable dishes and her penchant for well-constructed, fashionable, and made-to-last clothes. Her drive to educate us and to inculcate in us a love for learning had mixed results. We absorbed that love as children. But on reaching adolescence, all three of us rebelled in our own way, thwarting the educational paths our mother had intended.

Our mother read to us until she taught us to read and write. Vicky was five at the time and I was two years younger. Eager for knowledge, I couldn't wait until I reached Vicky's age, the age when I would be taught to read. So I learned alongside my sister. I loved stories. I loved to be read stories. And the idea that stories could come from a simple page of symbols, that all I had to do was associate the sounds of language with letters and a group of letters for everyday words, fascinated me. Merely arranging letters to make words for things, actions, conceptual images, then arranging these words to express my deepest thoughts or to tell an imagined story or a story of what happened to me that day, was a wonder, like magic. I felt as if I were on one side of a fence, gazing with longing through the slats at the other side, seeing people absorbing thoughts and ideas, chuckling to themselves, or crying for no seeming reason, and learning tasks just by looking inside a book. Others, with pens or pencils, scribbled on paper, page after page. I was locked out, until one day I learned how to understand the symbols. Then I took out the key from my pocket and opened the gate.

"When I learn to read," I told myself, "I'll read stories whenever I feel like it, not just when my mother can read to me." Vicky and I had a complete set of Golden Books that my mother read from. So entrenched was I in those fantastical stories of Little Red Riding Hood, Snow White, and Cinderella, that as soon as I mastered reading about Dick and Jane and Spot, I read my Golden Books with little difficulty and with newfound joy.

Vicky's and my formal education began with homeschooling, our mother teaching us from a curriculum provided by a school in Baltimore. I wanted to go to a local school with other kids, but my mother had chosen homeschooling long before we were of school age. Years later, when tía Sylvia told me that my mother had no confidence in Chilean doctors, I deduced that, likewise, she had placed no trust in the public schools to educate us. Moreover, my parents could not afford the tuition for private school at that time. Nevertheless, I found that I liked homeschooling. I liked the closeness of our teacher-student relationship. I liked the devotion she held for teaching and learning. Homeschooling provided my mother with a way to express her love for my sister and me.

My mother's penchant for reading and words was contagious. Once I learned to write well enough, I took on, as a special homework project, writing and making a book. It was a simple story about a dog and a child, illustrated and colored with my twenty-four-stick Crayola set. I cut the paper down to a manageable size—perhaps three or four inches square—used colored construction paper for the cover, punched two holes through the left side of the pages, and attached them all together with two bronze button clips. The Baltimore school gave me extra credit for my writing project. And, I pleased my mother. I wanted to make her happy.

After a couple of years of homeschooling, I entered the third grade of a British all-girls' school, St. Margaret's, in the seaside town we were living in then, Viña del Mar. At the start of every school day, the students assembled in their respective classrooms and, as the teacher entered, we stood up from our desks calling out in unison, "Good morning, Mrs. _____." Down we sat, then up again to sing "God Save the Queen." Anyone walking the halls of the school could hear this morning routine as a round of singing voices.

Our classroom had no clock. When the teacher needed to know the time, she would call on a student to walk down the hall where a large clock hung on the wall at the top of the stairs and come back to report the time to the class. Every girl had to take her turn in this errand. Early in my first semester of school my turn came. Being the new girl in class provided no excuse. I felt the rising heat of perspiration when she called on me. Telling time was not one of the lessons I had learned well at home. I walked out of the classroom, head down, resigned to the assigned task. But soon I looked up and around in awe. I was in the empty upstairs hallway, so beautiful, with such a tall ceiling and the afternoon sunlight spreading its soft yellow light on the wood-paneled walls. I walked down the great hall to meet the large clock at the top of a grand, ornate staircase, with antique balustrades etched by bug holes and a wide banister polished by years of hands and, when teachers weren't looking, by tiny bodies gliding down its length.

I stared at that big clock: *To read time, will looking intently help me? Will the clock reveal its message if I just concentrate hard enough?* I only felt the heat rushing again to my face as I walked back to the classroom to announce, "The little hand is on the three and the big hand on the six." I heard barely contained laughter. Time stopped there for me. And so does my memory of the following moments. Later, upon arriving home, I urgently demanded that my homeschooling mother teach me how to tell time.

My third-grade teacher, Mrs. Collier, practiced a punitive method of discipline. Every student in her class had a turn with Mrs. Collier at one time or another. If any girl misbehaved, she had to go to the front of the class to receive Mrs. Collier's accusation. From the girl, a weak protest: "But Mrs. Collier, I didn't mean to . . ." No matter. Mrs. Collier would take her by the shoulders and vigorously shake her back and forth. I can't imagine what our teacher intended to accomplish by this; perhaps she thought she could pry us loose of our misdeed? Humiliated and uncomfortably disoriented, the girl would walk the long way back to her seat. I too fell victim to Mrs. Collier's discipline. She called me to stand in front of the class. "Put your hands out, palms down." Whack! Whack! Several times she rapped my fingers with her wooden metal-edged ruler. Ouch!

Nevertheless, I loved going to school. I liked learning and making new friends and playing games. A photograph I still have reminds me of that happy time: my two best friends and I kneeling side-by-side on our school's grass field, smiling so naturally at the camera. Three little girls dressed alike, pockets stuffed with—what?—so happy to be together on a warm spring day.

The St. Margaret's school uniform delighted me: a short pleated gray woolen skirt, red wool blazer with the school's emblem sewn at heart level, and, for spring, a pastel-colored twill cotton skirt and a straw hat with an upturned brim. I kept that hat, along with the photo.

My time at St. Margaret's was short. After a couple of years, in 1956 our family moved from Viña del Mar to Chile's capital, Santiago, a two-hour drive inland. My father had procured a teaching assignment at the University of Chile there. My mother enrolled my sister and me in Santiago College, a private, primary-through-secondary-grades all-girls school founded in 1880 by American Methodist missionaries. Santiago College was the same school where my mother had taught years earlier.

Admission to Santiago College required passing the school's entrance exam. One question from that test stands out to me. The schoolmistress, or principal, a buxom, gray-haired, gray-suited Englishwoman, asked me, "Does the sun rise from the east or west?" I had no idea. A sense of direction was not then, nor would it ever be, part of my consciousness. I looked out the window for a clue, but there was none. I had a fifty-fifty chance of giving her the right answer or the wrong one. By the look that the schoolmistress gave me at my answer, I knew my choice was the wrong one. I also knew that from that moment, I would never forget this question or its answer. Yet I passed.

As in St. Margaret's, Santiago College uniforms were mandatory. In winter we wore dark green wool dresses with washable and removable white collars and cuffs. I needed help attaching these stiff accessories to my uniform, the buttons being way too big for the small unyielding buttonholes. "Vicky! I can't button these on! I guess I just can't go to school today." I would plop myself down on my twin bed. And here she'd come, with her deft little fingers working the buttons into place.

Over our dry-clean-only wool dresses we wore crisp white pinafores. Every Monday morning, the students arrived at school with freshly laundered, starched, and ironed collars, cuffs, and pinafores, which by Friday were limp, gray, and wrinkled. At times, our pinafores did not last the whole week without being laundered—such as that morning when our teacher led our class in single file, across the campus paths to another building on the campus, my stomach aching and churning as we walked under the hot sun. With caution I stepped gingerly so as not to stir the contents of my stomach needlessly. I was too embarrassed to let the teacher or any of my classmates know that I didn't feel well. Step by careful step until I could no longer contain the rush rising up my insides into my mouth. Whoosh! Out came my breakfast, the white pinafore absorbing the projected contents on their way down, but keeping my wool uniform intact.

An early, prescient dream haunts me. It speaks to my enduring longing for a demonstrative, affectionate parent, one whose faraway absence would come all too soon and another who would remain present but distant, closed to my need for comforting, reassuring love: *It is summertime and I am so happy to be here: my cousins, aunts and uncles are all here, like every summer, at our grandparents' fundo. We get to be with family, to play, swim, ride horses, have lots of adventures. Pick fresh raspberries. Go through thick brambles to fill our baskets with ripe, red, juicy berries. Eat them all, return with empty baskets. Spend the rest of the afternoon in bed, sick to our stomachs.*

Today is the day to go to town—all of my cousins are going. Lim-ache—a village full of fun, where we'll breathe in the rich aromas of bread baking and listen to street vendors calling out, sing-song, the produce they have for sale in their hand-drawn carts. "Lechu-u-ugas. Toma-a-tes, pata-ta-ta-tas!" Perhaps we'll have a chance to ride one of the horse-drawn Victoria carriages prancing down the main street. My cousins call out to me: "Vivian, we're going, are you coming?" "No," I say. I want to—I really, really do—but I'm not going to go . . . I want them to really want me to go with them. "Please, Vivian, come with us, we're about to leave." "No, I want to stay here." "But you'll be the only one left here." I want to go with them, but I don't want to go. "I'm staying here." Then it's quiet; everyone but a few adults is gone. I have no one to play with. I'm the only one left. I'm by myself.

I remember another early dream, which, like the earlier one, foretells a lasting characteristic. This dream seems to arise from its predecessor by recalling my stubborn self-denial, which ultimately leads to my sense of abandonment:

I am alone in my grandparents' farmhouse. It is evening, dark outside. I am in a large wood-paneled room with high, high ceilings. It's not a room I know. Where have I wandered to in my beloved grandparents' house? The windows are so near the ceiling that I need to bend my head way back to see out. I look up to the window on my left and see a large horse's head with wild eyes looking straight at me. I turn to the other wall and up to its window, and there, another horse is looking at me, creepy-like. How many of these larger-than-life-size animal monsters are outside, just on the other side of the walls? I'm scared; I don't want to be alone; why did my family all leave me behind? I want to be with them, with my abuelita, and with my mommy.

My years in Chile remain in my mind as memory snippets— fleeting images, a sprinkling of thoughts and physical sensations, a word or two. In an instant, a fragment touches a feeling buried deep inside and then passes by, leaving only a distant trace in its wake. To make sense of these visitations, I build stories around them. Soon, more memories waken. Lost scenarios appear. Details may not be accurate, but their emotional impact is real.

Pieces of my childhood bounce around my head:

Looking up to the tall poplars swaying in the wind, their leaves rustling high above my head.

Walking on a sunny path, hand in hand with my best friend.

Silky, soapy water running down my tiny baby body as tender hands bathe me in the bathroom sink.

Splashing in rain puddles with my rubber boots, then wading through the rivulets running toward the nearest storm drain.

Vicky and I preparing for bed, putting on matching baby-doll pajamas, just off my mother's sewing machine.

Sleeping through the day, too sick for school, counting figures on the drawn curtains and waiting for warm, healing soup to soothe the soreness in my throat.

Waking to the sweet tangy smell of mandarin marmalade on warm buttered toast.

Trundling through spiny bushes to pick ripened raspberries, only to come back empty-handed with telltale traces of red viscous liquid on my face and on my new white blouse.

Swimming and horseback riding and playing house and playing tag with my favorite cousins on our annual summer vacation gathering at the fundo.

Immersing myself in the birthday party that my mother has prepared for me, full of games, decorations, and pastel-frosted cupcakes.

Discovering the alphabet and making words with alphabet soup.

Moving my pencil within horizontal lines to create pairs of letters in cursive, one as a capital and its companion in lower case.

Opening my pencil box to its cache of neatly stored soft-lead pencils, an eraser, a pencil sharpener, and a few colored pencils, then choosing the right implements for my classroom workbook lesson.

Playing jacks, moving through the evermore complex series of throws with my classmates during recess.

Feeling my abuelita's warmth and her protective arms surrounding me as I sit on her lap and lay my head on her soft bosom. Abuelita, the gentle matriarch of our family, our idol.

"I love all my grandchildren. But you, Vivian, I love the best." This is what Abuelita disclosed to me during one of those snuggling embraces. Only a child, yet being recognized as someone unique, worthy of a special love, fulfilled me. It gave me a sense of belonging to a safe place. I've kept her words tucked in the folds of my brain; they have nurtured me throughout the years.

Not until sixty years later, long after Abuelita's death, would I understand the value of her words. On one of my return trips to Chile, at a lunch that my cousins hosted, we talked about our time together as children, about our summers on the farm and our mutual love for our abuelita. Each of us loved her unconditionally and she loved all of us. "But I remember," I boasted to my cousins, "her telling me that she favored me, her little gringa, above all the others." All my cousins laughed with joy as I heard Eugenia, the one closest to me in age, say, "She said the same thing to each one of us!" "Oh . . ." Then I laughed too. They had seen, and I finally saw, the wide expanse of our abuelita's heart, where each of us had held a special place. As grown women we are grateful for the sustenance her love provided each of us during our formative years. How can you begrudge that?

I was not such a good kid. Oh, I seemed to be: an innocent face, round and chubby, cute—"Round like the full moon, see?" my abuelita would tell me. But I was mischievous and, in my opinion, had a guilty heart that didn't match my innocent face. Abuelita, I should have told you that the moon is hardly ever full; on every night of the month except one, shadows cover it.

My shadow self appears in one of my earliest memories: *But-terflies, of all colors: large black ones, small yellow ones, pale blue, oranges, reds surround me in my grandmother's garden. The rest of the world melts away. I am mesmerized by butterflies, their shifting, jerky movement in the air, their gentle landing on an open blossom, waiting, full with pollen. As the child calms at the breast, so does the butterfly absorb itself in its pollination task. Rhythmically, lan-guidly, it flutters its wings, down and up, in satisfaction.*

I was a small child when my parents gave me an insect collection display case. My grandmother's garden presented all sorts of bugs that ended up there. I captured beetles, bees and even butterflies, and put them in a canning jar with rubbing alcohol–soaked cotton balls at the bottom. Once they no longer had life left in them, I pinned their bodies to the corkboard in my case, each with its own label, in neat little rows.

Once I took a shortcut, by skipping the killing jar. I had caught a butterfly, a large black beauty with multicolored stripes and spots. I gently cupped it in my left hand and, with my right, chose one of the spare pins I kept at the inside edges of my case. With pin in hand I pierced my black beauty's thorax, then stuck the butterflied pin onto the corkboard. I watched her flutter, frantically—rainbow dust flying off in every direction—until she could flutter no more.

My dark act of malice planted itself in my moral consciousness. My young child's mind reflected on the cruelty of my action. I won-dered where this dark impulse came from and why. Wickedness, I decided, fluttered inside me.

Still a child, but older, I joined three of my boy cousins in their play. I liked being with the boys; they took risks, they played boldly. It was the end of summer; our grandparents' swimming pool had just been drained. We cousins, siblings, aunts, and uncles had spent our summer together at the fundo, and now it was time to return to our homes in the city. My male cousins and I descended the pool ladder into an empty cemented well, where just a few days earlier we had run and jumped splashing into its cool deep water. Our voices resonated and echoed as they bounced off the walls. Happy frogs leapt and chirped in the newly vacated space; the only water remaining lay in puddles formed by imperfections in the swimming pool's floor.

One of the cousins challenged us to a game: "See if you can throw a frog against the wall hard enough to make it splatter," he said. Each of us had a turn. At eight years old, I wasn't strong. But with the force of my throw, the frog exploded against the cement wall. A burst of colors from my frog's insides broke through the tender skin of its underbelly, painting the wall with oozing butter and lemon yellow, olive green, and brown to black. I was sickened. End of game. "Stop," I said. "Let's not play at this anymore." I'm a sissy, I thought, and I don't care.

My cousins may have forgotten this late summer afternoon game. They may even have played it again the next summer. But not with me. Splattered frog images haunted me.

And still, my dark impulses rose again. My brother would forget the nosebleed episode, but I could not. The force of my eleven-year-old anger put such power into my arms shaking his shoulders back and forth that they caused his little button nose to erupt. First blood, then tears. He was only five years old, for heaven's sake! Just because he didn't follow my instruction? Or didn't clean up his room as he was told to do so? Maybe he left a mess in the kitchen? The cause is hardly significant, but the effect was. *He doesn't deserve this treatment*, I thought on seeing what I had done, *no matter what the reason, no matter that nosebleeds come easily to him*. "I'm sorry! Oh, Jimmy, I'm so sorry! I didn't mean to . . ."

What terrible deeds clouded my heart? Childhood mischief mostly, hardly worth noting. But at the time, every misdeed gave evidence of my flawed self. I was spanked for transgressions my parents knew about. Their principle: Spank to teach the child her actions were wrong. Spanking was the right—no, the duty—of the parent. After all, the child should not be spoiled; that was worse. Better discipline the child so that she learns misbehavior is not acceptable. My mother spanked me with her hand. My father spanked me with his belt. Although neither parent ever used a stick, my sister and I wanted to make sure they never would. After one particular storm that left the backyard full of debris, we quickly picked up all the fallen tree limbs and tossed them over the fence. We cleared our yard of any potential weapons. But my father's belts, we wouldn't dare touch. They had to stay. My spankings were not so much about their admittedly negligible pain as they were about humiliation. They worked. They left me crying in remorse. I never felt I didn't deserve them.

On one of our annual summer sojourns to my grandparents' farm, a group of us cousins—all between seven and ten years old—took an afternoon walk on the less-familiar road across the highway from the farm. On the way home we came upon a dead snake on the path. "Let's have some fun. Let's take it back to tease the maid," said one of the boys. We all knew that this younger maid—the one who cleaned and washed, even made our beds—had what I would later describe as a phobic fear of snakes. Scaring her would be a hoot, our childish minds decided. Using a long stick, we lifted the limp snake and carried it back dangling from the stick. Not "we," actually; only one of the cousins dared to lift the dead weight of this abhorrent creature and walk with it flapping around so closely in front—what if it were only playing dead?

On arriving, a few of us entered the house and went into one of the large back rooms where the maid was. Another few of us, notably the one carrying the stick, stayed just outside the door. To which group did I belong? No matter, we all acted as one. After the maid greeted us and asked how we enjoyed the walk, we said, hardly able to contain our chuckles, that we had a surprise for her, something we had found and wanted to show her. She loved and trusted us, and so she showed pleasure at our enthusiasm.

Then the remaining couple of us entered the room, and whoever was holding that stick flung its dead weight onto the floor, the action causing the serpent to writhe and slide. Screams and laughter—it was hard to tell one from the other, who was screaming and who was laughing. But I had no trouble recognizing who was making the loudest, most bloodcurdling screams. I stood transfixed, in horror, at what we had done, what we were causing. Was I the culprit who had carried the stick and flung this slimy cadaver in here? It was all of us, each of us culpable in this heinous act.

"It's not alive! It's dead! There's nothing to worry about!" I shouted, we all shouted. We loved this good woman and did not want to cause her the pain we had unleashed. Laughter and screams evolved into tears. There we all were, realizing what we had done and begging forgiveness. The maid calmed down and forgave us, or said she did. Did she? We didn't deserve it. We should have been spanked instead, until black and blue.

Small bits of memories from long ago churn inside and stack up to form a prevailing impression: mine was a happy childhood in Chile. Surely a romantic image. An image formed from the day I left Chile, as unhappy remembrances began to sift away from my mind. My Chilean childhood became the foundation by which to measure my life and my world from then on. Not everyone is so fortunate to have had such a measuring stick.

The Break

By 1957, when my sister was ten, her genetic heart condition had reached a critical point. My parents faced a grave decision: the imminent death of their first child or a trip to the United States for her to receive the recently developed and not-yet-widely available open-heart surgery. Family offered to help with the expenses. My parents scheduled the surgery and made travel arrangements. Soon after they arrived in the United States, they took Vicky to Stanford, to meet with the pioneer in the development of open-heart surgery and Vicky's surgeon-to-be, Dr. Frank Gerbode. Happily for me, I stayed behind with my beloved abuelita during their months-long absence.

Both of my grandparents moved to Santiago to care for me while school was in session. My grandfather left the management of his fundo to Beto, one of his senior employees. Nono missed his land. Metropolitan life offered its attractions and lure, but none like the riches of the country.

After a successful operation and long recovery period, Vicky and my parents returned to Chile. Vicky went back to school with a newfound enthusiasm, although her stamina remained fragile. She focused more on her studies than on physical activities. With my friends I'd play ball and jump rope and skip. With my sister I'd play cards and Monopoly and jacks and dolls. We each had our own Barbie-like doll, Vicky's with dark hair, mine with light brown. They came with her from the States, each with two outfits—one casual and the other a frilly party dress—and tiny plastic high-heeled shoes. No stores in Chile sold outfits for Barbie-like dolls, so we implored our mother to sew outfits for them. "You have to learn to sew them yourself," she said simply. First, she taught us how to knit. Vicky made a wool cape for her doll. I managed to make a blanket for mine. She then taught us sewing basics. Vicky and I struggled but managed to use colorful remnants my mother had in her sewing basket and constructed some simple, one-piece garments.

In time, Vicky's condition worsened; her operation had not fully resolved her health issue. A year and a half after her surgery, Vicky once again found herself in great danger of losing her life. To receive a medical evaluation, she required another trip to the United States.

I cannot say that the tragedy of Vicky's congenital heart condition was an opportunity for change in my mother's life. Rather, it was a tragedy of confluence. There must have been much discussion between my parents about undertaking a venture they could surely not afford and the uncertainties it would bring to their lives. Would Vicky's condition require another surgery? Could a less invasive medical procedure fix her? And how long would we need to stay in the United States? Fear for Vicky's life and torment about the uncertain prospects for securing medical help for her haunted my parents. I was not privy to any of those conversations. My father's family, in particular, his father, our nono—insisted: saving Vicky's life was paramount.

And so came the pivotal turn of my life. At the end of 1958, I was a ten-year-old child when my mother, Vicky, Jimmy, and I departed Chile for the United States. Our journey would be temporary, I believed, enough time for Vicky's heart ailment to be resolved and for my mother to miss her husband. Then the four of us would return once again to our happy life in Chile.

I had known that my sister's weak heart affected her health—she could not sustain physical activity like the rest of us. She was delicate but fun-loving. She teased me; I teased her. She was a child, after all. But I was not aware of the seriousness of her situation. My parents and adult relatives shielded me from such information. I knew about her open-heart surgery in 1957. But I was not versed in the gravity of her medical condition. I was confident that my big sister would be mended and ready to bounce back into our life, full of vigor and health. All my parents told me was that we—my mother, brother, and I—were accompanying Vicky to the United States for treatment of her life-threatening heart condition. About our return, communication remained vague.

Although I counted on a speedy return to Chile, I also sensed a more uncertain future. The gnawing thought, that this move would be no short-term stay, brushed my mind. In Chile, we moved several times, from Limache to Viña del Mar to Santiago. I was used to leaving one home for another and even looked forward to all our household moves. But I was afraid of this one. I dreaded leaving my home in Chile and then mourned its absence: left behind were my father, Abuelita, cousins, aunts and uncles, and my idyllic childhood. From the start of an unasked-for, undesired turn, hindsight lent a golden glow to the familiar, now broken path, which I had no wish to end.

The flight from Santiago to San Francisco was my first. Physical sensations that came from being airborne—the low whine of engines whizzing in my head, the pressure and popping in my ears, and sounds of people maneuvering in an enclosed space—heightened my turbulent emotions of fear and apprehension about what was to come, and grief for what was behind me, as well as wonder and curiosity about new experiences. Someone—perhaps my mother—had given me a little red purse: plastic, box-shaped with a shoulder strap; my first purse. Its plastic skin was tightly shirred, forming a texture pleasing to touch. The purse had a little gold clasp on the top that I liked to open and close, just for the feel and sound of the clasp. Inside I had put a few treasures: one American penny and one nickel; a folded piece of paper containing the perfectly, beautifully scripted signature of the foreman of the fundo; a tiny silver-decorated perfume bottle that my abuelita had given me. My little red purse carried nothing else. It was mostly empty, waiting to be filled with the new treasures I'd find in the place I was to visit, just long enough for my sister to undergo whatever treatment was needed for her sick heart and subsequent recovery period. Then we would all return home.

After our arrival in the US, I recalled an incident shortly before we left that, at the time, struck me in an odd way: I am sitting on my father's lap; we are in the living room of our last rented house in Santiago. My father asks me if I'm looking forward to going to the United States. *"Sí, pero . . . no para mucho tiempo."* ("Yes, but . . . not for too long"). "Celia, did you hear that?" my father shouts to my mother in the kitchen. "Vivian says she doesn't want to stay in the United States." I hear only a muffled acknowledgment from the kitchen. Why isn't Papo coming with us? Afraid of an answer I don't want to hear, I draw a dark curtain over possible consequences for our family. Maybe, I think, we're not coming back at all.

The woman who greeted us at the San Francisco airport as we disembarked the Pan Am flight from Santiago was a tiny four-foot-eleven, the height my sister would achieve as an adult. I saw this short woman in a large brown coat with arms akimbo, gray curls, spunky, loud, and happy, waiting for us. Her daughter had come home. She didn't embrace and kiss us—that was not the American way at the time. She spread her arms around her daughter briefly, then looked at each of us with a large smile. She didn't act like a grandmother. She was not like the only grandmother I had known,

Abuelita. Abuelita would have taken us in her arms, teary-eyed, and kissed each one of us. I would have breathed in her talcum powder smell. This grandmother smelled like baked chicken.

The San Francisco International Airport terminal was the largest building I'd ever been in during my short life. We followed this odd grandmother down long, wide, and impersonal walkways. I wanted to stop and stare, to look up and around and listen to the echoing sounds of high heels on hard floors. I wanted time to take in the unfamiliar tones of my mother's language. But our grandmother wanted to waste no time getting to the baggage claim area and then to her car that would take us to her home in Sacramento.

It had been a long flight from Santiago to San Francisco, and then a nearly two-hour drive to Sacramento. Lying in the back seat, I counted telephone poles rushing across my view. Only ten or twelve passed by before I fell asleep. I slept the rest of the way. Then, waking up in the dark of night, when the car stopped, I looked out the window to what would be our home.

I was not prepared for the over-the-top seasonal ornamentation I found in Sacramento. When we arrived late on Christmas Eve 1958, I was fascinated and bedazzled. Chile had treated the holiday with festivity, although with a more sober face: the ubiquitous but modestly decorated and lighted Christmas tree; a crèche, set up in the fireplace (no need for a fire in the Southern Hemisphere summer); and gifts wrapped in decorated paper. But none of these outdoor lights and plastic Santa Clauses hauling large stuffed brown bags over their shoulders romping in front yards. We had no outdoor ornamentation in Chile.

Sacramento embodied those Norman Rockwell Christmases I later saw depicted on the covers of *Life* magazine: tinsel, lights, pine-scented wreaths and trees, sticky-sweet candy canes, ornate glass ornaments, and that one sprig of red-ribboned mistletoe hanging high over front doorways waiting for the unsuspecting handsome caller. Dark, cold nights misted with such thick fog that colored lights draped over roofs and windows and doors glowed with halos.

Entering my grandmother's Sacramento house on that Christmas Eve, I was greeted by festive glitter, elaborately decorated packages, a tinsel- and icicle-laden tree, its branches bowed down by the weight of hanging ornaments. The centerpiece on my grandmother's dining room table held me in fascination: two white Styrofoam sleighs, adorned with red and green and gold sparkles, driven by reindeer caught in a mid-air leap. Small, red-striped mint-flavored candy canes were embedded in the tops of the Styrofoam sleighs. These Christmas figurines seemed to frolic on the red tablecloth and brought a little joy of welcome to my siblings and me.

The next morning, my new grandmother, my mother, Vicky, Jim, and I gathered around the heavily ornamented and garlanded tree to open presents. My mother gave my sister and me twin winter coats, an ice blue one for me and a pale rose pink for Vicky. I wasn't used to pastel-colored coats, having until then worn only dark neutral wool colors. These new coats of ours were made not from wool but from synthetic fibers. They looked, and felt, like cotton candy.

Christmastime in Sacramento was taken seriously. Other holidays were too—Halloween and Thanksgiving made their mark on the city's look—but Christmas was the most festive, the most decorative. The period from the late '50s to the early '60s was a time before the advent of serious commercialism and shopping mall come-ons lying in wait until just after the Halloween candy went on sale for half-price.

No matter that snow never fell on Sacramento. The only sleigh bells heard on streets came from "Jingle Bells" recordings accompanying department-store window scenes. Never having experienced real sleighs, a snow-deprived populace could only imagine visions of sleigh bells and reindeer dancing to the rings of a Salvation Army bell soliciting donations.

My grandmother, my mother, and her sister, Aunt Helen, all carried a tradition of holiday spirit with fanfare and flair. Aunt Helen and her two little girls spent weeks painting and decorating butcher paper and embellishing ribbons with sequins and glitter for wrapping their Christmas presents. My mother, with her two girls, cut out tissue-paper snowflakes and glued them to the front window with rubber cement. Our three-year-old brother, Jimmy, helped hang silver icicles on the bottom branches of the tree, while Vicky and I carefully unwrapped delicate glass ornaments held in beds of tissue, each stored in its own separate compartment of a sectioned box.

From a string above the mantel we draped our Christmas cards, and below the mantel above the hearth we hung our stockings. The three of us—my mother, my sister, and I, but not little Jimmy—constructed stockings from green and red felt and multicolored sparkles and sequins and white lace trim. One each for Vicky, Vivian, Jimmy, and Mommy.

On our first Christmas Eve in Sacramento, the infusion of magic and illusion astounded and delighted me. In my grandmother's house, my eyes moved from the table setting to the television in the living room. I had never seen a TV before. Looking closely at the screen images, I saw vibrating gray and white lines. I looked still closer and saw a million black and white dots. Like newsprint, except these dots jumped around and glowed, magically.

My mother, who, newly married, had left her country with expectations of splendor in Chile, returned with dismay on that Christmas Eve but was ready to take back what she had lost. I, who had no desire to leave my country to live in hers, was dazzled by the ostentation I found. The newness of my experience greeted me with surprise and wonder and helped offset my pain for what we had left behind.

Gradually, I learned how to recognize and reach through and beyond the glitter. I still marveled at dancing colored lights, reindeer figurines leaping in front yards, and Santa balloons waving in the cold winter wind. They still greeted me with joy, but I came to see the glitter for what it was rather than for what it promised.

Grandma Stevens had a toughness of will and strength of body resulting from what she called "elbow grease." She was lively, active, with a no-nonsense attitude. I laughed every time she hopped in the car to drive us anywhere.

From the back seat I see the driver's-side door open and watch her purse fly over the front seat to plunk down and settle on the passenger's side of the bench-style seat. Nice shot, Grandma, I say to myself. As always, her purse lands right where she intended it to go. Next, in comes my grandmother, all four feet eleven inches, in one movement and plops down on the driver's seat. We are ready to go. My grandmother turns on the ignition, then maneuvers the gear shift—not a stick shift but the kind with the lever on the steering column—and with elbow grease, shifts into gear. We are going downtown to the department stores to shop. I don't like to shop. Too much taking off and putting on; boring. It's too hot to try on fall sweaters and scratchy wool dresses. They don't even look good on me. At least Grandma will take us to lunch, where I can have a BLT with a milkshake. And then we'll head for home, where I can run through the lawn sprinklers. And before that, I get to enjoy a more elaborate car entry routine: Not only will Grandma hurl her purse over the front seat, but so too will I see her newly purchased packages follow in flight—one after the other in perfect rhythm.

Grandma Stevens drove a salmon-colored Ford, perhaps a 1956 model, until the late 1960s. I've never seen that color on any other car before. Hers was a modest, well-running car. Luxury did not attract this practical woman. Machine design and appearance were of no significance. Functional value, neatness, and cleanliness took larger roles. And so did her character: get the job done, do what's needed to get it right, take care of the functional details. Do not take or do it for adulation, thanks, or praise. Just do it.

She was a long-standing widow. Her husband, James, had died suddenly of a heart attack in 1929. She was thirty-six at the time, with three young children. My mother, the eldest of the three, was twelve.

Was it a job opportunity in San Diego that lured my grandmother away from New Jersey, where her husband, a US Naval Air Force lieutenant, had been stationed? Or did she yearn to start her new life in unfamiliar territory nearly three thousand miles away? Little did she know that she would set an example for her daughter, who would surpass her bold move nearly ten years later. Grandma accepted the job in San Diego as a high school teacher, teaching science. She then left that job to enter a lifetime career in social welfare. After ten years with the County of San Diego, in 1938, she was offered a position with the State of California's welfare department in Sacramento. She packed up her family, moved to Sacramento, and stayed.

Grandma Stevens was a woman with a social conscience and commitment to others. After she retired from her career in social work, she became a contributor and active participant in UNICEF. She was a world traveler and a woman who had raised three young children and lived comfortably on her own as a widow. She didn't need assistance but gave it to others. Even though finances were not openly discussed in her household, Grandma financially helped my mother when she arrived in the States with three children and without her husband. I later discovered that my grandmother never expected to be repaid.

From family members I've learned that Grandma visited Chile while we lived there. I had forgotten. Was I too young? Did I understand that she was my mother's mother? I already had a grandmother I loved, Abuelita, and had no need for another one.

I knew the two Barbie-like dolls, which were only available in the US and not in Chile, were gifts to my sister and me from our American grandmother. I loved my doll; she was my companion until I was ten years old. As with all my Chilean childhood treasures, my American doll stayed behind when we left for the US. Only after our move would I come to know the woman who gave her to me as a grandmother.

From the time we arrived at the end of 1958 until my mother found employment and a house to rent, we lived with Grandma Stevens in her Sacramento house on Seventh Avenue. And, soon enough, we lived with her again for nearly another year in 1960–1961 when my mother became ill with TB and was sent to a sanatorium. I was twelve and thirteen at the time, and not an easy daughter-granddaughter. My grandmother had a handful with me; Vicky, who was two years my senior; and Jimmy, seven years younger. Retired since 1956 for only four years, living on her own, visiting her children and grandchildren on her own time, Grandma now had to reassume the role of single mother to my mother's children.

Our grandmother saw to our needs, provided for us, made sure we completed our chores, disciplined us, loved us. She was affectionate and caring in her own way, but not in a cuddly, indulgent abuelita-like way. Grandma was concerned about our well-being and proper upbringing but not in a demonstrative way. Much like her daughter, Celia.

But we had to have been a burden to her during the eight months my mother was hospitalized—especially me, the difficult child. I still deeply felt the effects of my separation from my home country and now the loss of my mother's care, and I struggled with assimilation into my new environment. Grandma was forgiving when I told her that I no longer wished to accompany her, Vicky, and Jimmy on the weekly Sunday visits to my mother in the sanatorium. I preferred spending time with my newly made friends. She did not demand my presence; she put up with my surly and uncooperative behavior.

If she knew of those summer evenings in my twelfth year when I sneaked out after bedtime to meet my girlfriend, she would, I was sure, reprimand me. Our nighttime wanderings were innocent yet, in retrospect, potentially dangerous. Sue and I spent those night hours walking the neighborhood, talking, going to the schoolyard just to play jacks on the asphalt under the courtyard lights, and never considered possible dangers. I was only too happy to have found a best friend, a soul mate, in this foreign environment. I received no reprimands from Grandma for my nighttime outings.

"Your grandmother told me she saw you leaving the house at midnight, after you and Vicky had gone to bed; you can't be trusted!" my mother said after she returned from the hospital. Oh, really? I thought, Grandma never said anything to me.

Grandma wanted the best for me when she enrolled me in a charm school. I was a twelve-year-old tomboy who felt alienated from the surrounding social structure. Why not, I thought, learn proper girl-like manners? Maybe I'd learn to be more like the other Sacramento kids. I had been struggling to hide my Chilean character and mannerisms, so alien to them, so private for me.

On my first day at charm school, my classmates and I learned the proper way for a lady to sit from a standing position: place both feet together—keeping the knees together at all times, of course—

and then bend at the knees and hips while lowering yourself, slowly, to the seat behind you. As you sit, turn your legs—both legs still together—slightly to the left so that your lower body position is oriented at an angle but your shoulders and head face forward. Fold your hands on your lap. Do not fidget. The act of sitting took skill and practice. It felt awkward. I teetered in my movement down to the chair, which I hoped was in position to receive my tensed buttocks. I was not allowed to turn my head to look. Our teacher asked if any of us had physical features we wished to mask, features that made us feel self-conscious. "Yes," I said, "I have knock-knees." "Well, that's easy to fix," she said. "All you have to do is stand with your right leg slightly in front of the left one, like this," she demonstrated by placing my legs in position as I faced the full-length mirror. "See, now your right knee overlaps the left, allowing your legs to stand together with no gaps. And yes, you will need to practice sitting from your new standing position."

I never went back for class two. "Grandma," I pleaded, "I don't want to go to that school. I can't do what those other girls do, I don't belong in their crowd, I don't go to their parties." Grandma was disappointed, but she understood, or just relented. That was the end of charm school for me. And when my teenage years came, my tomboy behavior ended too.

Grandma Stevens kept her thoughts and feelings hidden. I never saw her face betray anything other than resolute calm during emotional moments. I wonder whether she resented her son-in-law while never even whispering a word of disapproval or disdain. My father could not support his family, neither financially nor with his presence. How much did Grandma know about her daughter's relationship with him, their marriage, and even my father's character? Not for me to be told. There never was talk of my father, at least none that reached my ears. I can only imagine a scenario in the early years of my parents' physical separation:

My mother, reading a letter from her husband, in her room. My grandmother arrives at our house to take her to dinner, earlier than expected. Grandma hears soft, muffled crying as she lets herself in the front door. The crying stops abruptly. "Celia, are you there?" Some noises can be heard from my mother's bedroom. "Yes, I'll be out in a minute." Sounds of sorrow dissolve into irritation: "You're half an hour early!" A few minutes later, my mother enters the living room, her face washed clean of makeup, a reddish puffiness around her eyes. "Celia, what's wrong?" asks my grandmother. "Oh nothing, just aller-gies this time of year!" A forced smile. My mother's on edge, almost angry, impatient. "Oh, Mother," she says, "can't you see I wasn't ready just yet? I still have to dress, put my makeup on. You'll just have to sit and wait for me!" My mother goes back into her room and slams the door behind her. Her mother knows: something's not right. She sees an opened envelope on the end table among other papers and unopened mail: tissue-thin blue with red and blue diagonal stripes along the edges and a large red "Correo Aéreo" stamped on the diagonal next to her daughter's name and address. Without needing to consult the undecipherable return name and address written on the upper left edge, she knows. A stream of irritation seeps through her mind. She walks to her daughter's bedroom door and knocks quietly. She dis-appears through the opening, now closing, door. The door to my own imagination closes too.

Whatever conversation took place between them regarding my mother's sorrow, or my mother's anger, or the injustice of her situ-ation, or the failing hopes of her marriage, and life's unpredictable circumstances, opinions about my father and his situation must have been discussed behind those closed doors in my imagined scene. I was too young, too wrapped in my own yearning for my lost past, too shut off from my mother's sorrows to delve into them.

I did not consider whether she regretted her move back to the US, whether she anticipated a lonely life here, or whether she held on to a hope that her husband would join her. My child's mind had concluded that she intended to remain in the US from the time we left Chile, whether or not our father would follow. Why else would she have brought all three of her children here?

Even so, I couldn't have guessed the depth of my mother's emotions. She never expressed them in my presence. And neither did my grandmother veer from presenting a stoic image to the children of her grieving daughter. Either my mother was unsuited for Chile, or Chile was unsuited for her. Either circumstance would lead to the grief that comes from the loss of love.

I Want to Go Back to Chile

In my first school semester in Sacramento, I remained silent during the daily recital of the Pledge of Allegiance and occasional singing of "The Star-Spangled Banner." At first I didn't understand the words. Then I learned to mouth them, keeping silent. I had to stay in the US, but I didn't have to be "American."

Soon after we arrived in my mother's home country, I wanted to go back to my father's and mine. *"Yo quiero ir a Chile,"* I wrote in tiny handwriting inside the walk-in closet that Vicky and I shared at Grandma Stevens's house. I inscribed these words to the left of the closet door, on wainscoting at my ten-year-old eye level. My cursive, vertically oriented letters, so small, barely decipherable, written for . . . whom? My mother? Maybe it was meant just for my eyes, yet hoping someone would discover this hidden message. Like placing a message in a bottle and throwing it out to sea. I wanted to believe that by recording my most deep-seated wish, it could come true. I needed to release this bottled-up longing from inside me.

I could not tell the only person who could make my wish come true: my mother. I sensed an implicit, unstated taboo preventing me from speaking of a return. My sister's health loomed over us. Guilt silenced my self-indulgence. I wanted to scream the words out to my mother, "I want to go to Chile!" But I could not speak what my heart felt. Still, I expected her to know. I thought she could tell by my sullen attitude and growing resentment. And if I were to break the silence to say, "I want to go to Chile; when will we go home?" I feared what the answer might be.

Our closet, opening into the living room and under the stairs, was my secret refuge. I stored my secrets there. Walk in, close the door, pull the little chain hanging from the light above the door to turn on the light, then pull it again to turn it off to let only the scant ray of light creeping under the door to illuminate my darkness. Alone inside the closet I could think, sulk, cry, muffling my sobs with clothing. I could think of my country, my family and friends. I could plan my escape. Inside the closet I indulged my sorrow, my grief for lost happiness. I'd reach far into the closet depths to take out a few cherished possessions I had brought with me—a St. John and the Dragon medallion on a small gold chain that my abuelita had given me for protection, a letter from my father, a grosgrain ribbon I used to wear when I had braids—grieve over them, then return them to their hiding places.

I missed everything I no longer had. We had brought little with us on our six thousand–mile flight, only clothes and toiletries. No Chilean or family mementos; no toys, treasures, or secret possessions; not even my favorite two dolls had accompanied me. We left all that mattered behind. Inside the closet, I enumerated the losses and dwelled on broken hopes.

Many years later I heard about a trunk for Vicky and me in which such things as our dolls, school workbooks, photographs, childhood treasures, and clothing were stored, awaiting our return to Chile. But our childhoods were long gone by the time either one of us came back; and then, we came only as visitors. Our trunk was not there.

Gone, like Lulubelle, the duck I took on as a pet when I was five or six. Lulubelle: I named her after a Disney bear character. Not that I liked the Disney bear or the Disney film about her. I just liked the name, the dancing *l*'s: Lu-lu-belle. My duck, known in Spanish as *pato mudo* (mute duck), must have been a Muscovy, a type of duck valued for its succulent flesh. And, among the Muscovies, the visually appealing white breeds are the preferred choice for diners. Lulubelle was of the white variety. For one long summer at my grandparents' fundo, she was my pet duck. She could pick me out of a crowd and, making her muffled grunting noises, waddle away from her companion ducks right up to me. I must have been there when she cracked out of her shell, imprinting onto her newly hatched duck brain.

The next summer, no duck waddled toward me and no duck answered my desperate call: "Lulubelle! Lulubelle!" I asked my mother, "Where is Lulubelle?" and my abuelita, *"¿Dónde está Lulú?"* "She's not here right now." "When will she be back?" Evasive answers were all I received. Then I understood her farm-to-table fate. "We didn't know Lulubelle was among them; we forgot."

That trunk, too, was forgotten, eaten up by time and stashed away or thrown out. I never learned its true fate. But I know I didn't have the chance to claim it in time.

Of all she left behind, I wonder what she, my mother, missed most of all when she returned to the US, after more than a dozen years in Chile, settling into marriage, growing a family there, adjusting to the culture, then going right back to the home she left when, by marrying a Chilean, she had started that whole journey. Would she have known then, or even suspected, that she would never return? And that she would never retrieve anything of her life there nor reclaim any relationship she had cherished? Perhaps she forgot about those things, those intimates, that adopted country, now abandoned. She never mentioned them to me after we left; she hardly acknowledged their existence.

What things were forgotten? Her set of china, patterned with a single, simple long-stemmed rose; the drapes she made for the living room, their fabric of green and ivory shades and large tulips in vertical rows; the paintings on the wall—Degas's dancer backstage dressed in yellow tulle, her upper body bent forward for a full leg stretch before the dance; my mother's Singer sewing machine; our record collection; everything that contributes to the living that a family does in a home. And her husband and her adopted family, my father's family, how easily she forgot, I thought at the time. She didn't talk of them, all left behind, forgotten. As if those thirteen years in Chile had never existed. Maybe she believed it would be better for us to move on, get on with our new life and forget what was behind us. She didn't say.

My Chilean childhood became my consolation. There in my memories I found comfort and solace while living in a world, if not inhospitable, then not welcoming. In Chile I belonged to a community and a large extended family. Here in the US I had few relatives, all distant to me. I was now the other, from a faraway, little-known, foreign, underdeveloped country. A novelty to the provincial attitudes of that time in Sacramento.

Vicky and I started school in February 1959. I entered the sixth grade in the elementary school near Grandma Stevens's house, and Vicky started the seventh grade in the junior high next door. On my first day, the homeroom teacher, Mrs. Janssen, stood with me at the front of the class. "Boys and girls, this is your new classmate: Vivian Pisano," pronouncing my surname as if it had a long *i* and a *z*: "Paizahno." "She's from Chile. Boys and girls, do you know where Chile is?" I looked out at the twenty-five faces looking at me, the alien, who was unacceptably different from them. A heavy silence filled the room. My face turned hot and red. Mrs. Janssen answered her own question: "It's a long, skinny country in South America.

Now Vivian," she said as she turned to me, "we will all want to hear about your country!" I wanted to melt down into the floor.

No one in my class knew anything about Chile at that time, nor did they seem to care to learn. I heard only questions meant to taunt. "Is it chilly in Chili?" "Are you a *paisano* like "friend" in Italian?" Murmured laughter. I didn't want to tell them anything about my beloved, lost country.

Standing in front of the class, on display to a room full of strangers, I recalled an experience in Chile with the few Americans I knew. My mother was friends with an American couple, he in the US military. They had two daughters about the same age as Vicky and me. The family lived apart from the flotsam, as I imagined they considered *chilenos*, in a neighborhood of like-minded foreign families. On one particular visit to their house, the girls brought Vicky and me to their bedroom to show us all the wonderful US-made toys and clothes they had. The older girl, snooty and contemptuous, and her sister proudly displayed their latest dolls. We could only look, not touch. Vicky and I were not even allowed to sit on their twin beds neatly covered with matching white cotton chenille bedspreads. "Don't!! Don't you sit on the bed!" the older one screeched. "You'll ruin our new electric blanket from the States." What, no hot water bottles used in American homes?

And yet here I was, only a few years later, surrounded by Americans, in their home territory, ready to torment me for not being like them. I spoke their language—after all, my mother was, like them, American, and I had spoken only English with her for as long as I could remember—but mistakes in my pronunciation were noted with glee. In reading class, when my turn came up to read a passage out loud and I encountered an unfamiliar word, I'd follow English-language pronunciation conventions as I knew them. Coming across the word "Yosemite," I proudly stressed the first syllable and pronounced the last as the word "might." Jeers erupted from my classmates. A chuckle from the teacher preceded her slow parsing of Yosemite's correct pronunciation.

One day, after the school bell rang and we were all in our seats with no teacher present, we sixth graders couldn't help but fool around. It was our kid nature. One of the boys, Bobby Gomez (he was kind of cute, short like me, quick and smart), teased me. It felt like flirting. I got up and went up to his desk to punch him—lightly, playing—just as the sixth-grade teacher walked in. "Vi-vi-an!" sang the booming female voice. "Now we know!" Hoots and laughter exploded around me. *That's the end of that little game*, I thought, *but he is cute . . . and he's blushing too.*

I was accustomed to teasing and jostling by my Chilean classmates. I took part in those games. But in the US, taunts humiliated me. They reminded me of the foreignness I felt, as if I were subhuman and a safe target for mockery. I didn't want any focus on me. I just wanted to be like everyone else, a regular kid. But I felt they didn't want to let me in. So I learned to hide my alien background. "Let them pronounce my name however they want to," I'd say to myself. "I won't correct them. Just don't let them ask where I'm from, or about my accented English, or have them hear my secret Spanish language that I now speak only to myself."

I blush, look down, feel shame. For having such a name. For having a name that no one heard of before. For having a name that no one can pronounce. My name is not "Pai-sa-no," it's "Pisano," very simple. No drawn-out vowels, no z-sounding s, no embellished syllables. Just simple letters pronounced exactly as they appear. The letters don't pretend to be anything else. But I can't tell them.

I feel shame for being so different from everyone else. And I want to blend in, be like the others, with lots of friends, like I used to have back where I came from. But I'm not like them. I'm different. I can speak their language all right but accented, foreign-like. I'm trying to speak English the way they do, but I get teased every time I try to pronounce a word I don't know in the way I think it would be pronounced. I want to dress like them, look like them, laugh like them. I'm not like them. And I stick out like a sore thumb. Even my first name makes me stand out. No one else ever answers to "Vivian."

I took comfort by talking to myself, softly, so no one could hear me. My private conversation was in my native language, easy, natural, expressive. I thought no one was aware of my private mutterings.

Everyone lines up, walking two-by-two. I, as one, walk behind them, looking down, talking softly. "Oh Vivian!" the girl in front of me turns around to say, "you're talking to yourself! In Spanish! How swe-e-t! You sound so cute!" Others stop—they want to hear too. My face turns red. I can't think. That's it. No more chatting by myself. Break the habit. And speak only English in this English-only country. Be more like them and they won't tease me so much, I hope.

Alas, my foreignness went beyond language. My culture and mannerisms defined it too.

I didn't like this new, different world, where soup came ready-made straight from the can into a pot; where bread that "helps build strong bodies twelve ways," whose freshness you were encouraged to experience by squeezing the package, tasted like a cotton sponge that balled up and stuck to the top of your mouth. Cleaning solutions that promised to leave your floors and surfaces effortlessly "sparklin' clean!" only made you scrub harder and longer and leave you distressed over your inability to measure up to the beautiful TV housewife who had not even one disturbed hair on her perfectly coiffed head. I didn't belong and I didn't want to.

Lunchtime. It seems that every other kid's lunch box has a peanut butter sandwich wrapped in wax paper that their mother made this morning. I can smell those sandwiches as soon as they release the latch on their lunch box. I hate peanut butter. It sticks. I have to use my index finger to dislodge it from the top of my mouth. When no one's looking, that is. I don't even like the taste—oily and salty and dry. My mother makes me avocado sandwiches. These I like. It reminds me of the avocado on toast we had in Chile for breakfast and tea.

"Yuck! What is that black and green yucky paste in your sandwich? It smells! Eeyew!" I look at the lunch that my mother prepared for me this morning. I saw her cut into a nice ripe avocado, mash it up well with a fork into a bright green smooth paste, sprinkle a little salt, and spread it onto a thick slice of bread. Not that light white foamy stuff. Then, carefully, my mother laid another piece of bread on top and cut the whole thing in half, diagonally. Into a waxed paper sandwich bag and into my Roy Rogers metal lunch box. Then a banana to accompany it. Not a thermos of milk. I only like chocolate milk. So my thermos holds either chocolate milk, juice, or even the rare but delicious strawberry milk that Borden sells at this time. As I open my sandwich bag, I see that the avocado has discolored after a few hours in my lunch box. And the banana has ripened too, dark brown now, with a deep, rich aroma. Mmm! My sandwich and banana taste just as good as if I'd eaten them freshly prepared. Better, even. I'll go eat my avocado sandwich and ripened banana by myself, away from the heckling of others. Besides, I don't want to sit across from someone opening their mouth wide and slapping it closed, trying to keep the peanut butter from sticking to their palate. That's disgusting!

But teasing and bullying are not contained within one country's borders; taunting and being taunted are part of childhood. As I made my way in unfamiliar territory, I saw my classmates' bullying not as unique to them but rather as a common experience. If I'd only looked back a few years previously while I was still in Chile, I could have understood.

"Vee-vee-AN," I heard from the other side of the playground, the big girls' side. I was fairly new to Santiago College, in the fourth grade. The school's classroom buildings were separated on campus, one side for grammar school and the other for the middle and upper grades. But all students more or less shared the same schoolyard area for recess and games. The big girls, the ones in the higher grades, had more status. They intimidated us, the grammar school kids. Whenever our paths crossed, we little ones were subject to their taunts. So we kept to the side closest to our grammar school classrooms. The big girls kept to their own side too.

During this lunchtime period, I had become their target. What had I done? It had to be something they didn't like or approve of, something that gave them, the bigger girls, the right or duty to punish me. Laughing, walking toward me, the group of four or five girls seemed friendly, nothing to worry about, as I went about my business playing with my friends. I should have sensed that something was wrong. Why else would a group of high school girls come over to our side, pretending to enjoy cavorting with grammar school girls? One grabbed me, laughing; then they all pulled me away. I tried to resist. No one came to my rescue, not even any teachers. I looked around; there were no teachers in view. My tormentors took me to a bench on their side of the school quad. One sat down and pulled my face down onto her lap; then, with all of them helping her and laughing hysterically, they lifted up my skirt, exposing my pantied buttocks. The girl on whose lap I was perched spanked me until they all could laugh no more.

This spanking stung. I cried. My tears came not from pain but from the shame and humiliation I felt. And guilt, too. For what? What had I done to deserve a spanking? Did other grammar-school girls get the same treatment? The bell for class sounded, and the big girls left. As they walked away, I heard them say something about teaching me a lesson. I returned to the grammar school side and to my classroom without uttering a word.

Vicky's operation was successful; her life was saved. But we did not return to Chile. Our move to the US became permanent. My father remained in Chile. The why and how and when of the decision to stay here as a broken family were out of my reach. We had no such discussion.

At my new, American grammar school, I averted conversations about my background. I turned inward, longing for invisibility. To disappear. And so I did, in my mind, by removing myself from the scene to observe. Observe how they acted, their mannerisms, what they said, how they pronounced their words. I could hide behind my American appearance, but my mannerisms and awkward conversational English gave me away. To survive in the society where I was to stay, I aimed to assimilate and deflect attention from my native cultural identity. I learned how to avoid making a spectacle of myself and how to avoid being the one who got laughed at. Better to be seen through than to be seen. Keep quiet, speak like them, pretend to be like them. In time, my secret language faded away. English surfaced. I relaxed and let friendships in.

Insofar as my name, I would grow to like it, to laugh along with its sing-song variations and tolerate its mispronunciations. I lost my ardent desire to change it. Mispronunciations brought out the music in my name. When the vowels are stretched along a scale, there's a melody in it—"Pai-i-za-no-o."

My assimilation was, in fact, so very successful that after several years, I had forgotten my first language. Spanish slipped away from me slowly, hardly noticeable but, without practice, inevitably. As the language of my speech turned to English, so did the language of thoughts and dreams. Next to fall away was the intimate language between my sister and me, and then the Spanish taunts and endearments for my young brother. No language change was needed for communicating with my mother: she, as the American in our family, always spoke English with us and we with her.

With the language receding, so did pains of separation. Chile as the place I knew and loved and yearned to be back in, the longing for my school friendships and for family, were retreating, as was my old sense of self. I began to establish deep friendships here and ties to my environment. A new self was surfacing.

Television was what captivated my ten-year-old consciousness upon our arrival. I'd had no previous TV experience. I never knew any Chilean homes that had televisions. If they had been introduced in Chile before the 1960s, televisions would have been seen only in the more affluent homes.

However unfamiliar I was with this new technology, it took little time for me to become acclimated to it, and for it to lift the burden of my new life in the US.

What better way to spend a Saturday morning than snuggling with my sister, both of us in our PJs, on Grandma Stevens's Danish recliner to watch the weekly run of cartoons on her black-and-white TV? *Fractured Fairy Tales* and *Rocky and Bullwinkle* were among our favorites. The twists and turns and surprises in these stories captured us and left us in awe. And for me, it was an opportunity to question circumstances, to seek reassurance from someone who shared my world experience and, like me, now found herself ignorant of the ways of this foreign world. "Why," I'd ask my older sister, "Vicky, why did the . . . ?" "Vivian, stop nagging me and just think about it some more!"

Those other mind-numbing, cruel cartoons—*The Road Runner*, *Bugs Bunny*—we watched and tolerated, but without enjoyment and wonder. They all had the same, tired storyline: a character is beaten up, he subsequently appears decked out with Band-Aids, and then, in the next frame, he's good as new and seeking revenge. Not like real life at all, where the wounded are left without recourse to tend to their wounds. And not like real life where the unexpected intervenes, breaks your familiar path, and takes you in an unanticipated direction. Who would have imagined that Vicky and Vivian, at twelve and ten years old, would have been snuggling up in a Danish recliner watching Saturday morning cartoons in their American grandmother's home?

Vicky and I fit together just right on that recliner. Especially if I sat down first and claimed a slightly larger half of the seat. My sister indulged me. The recliner had two settings, upright and a 45-degree angle, perfect for viewing and for planting our feet on the matching stool. Two little girls captured by the magic of TV. After spending the week in unfamiliar schools, with unfamiliar customs, among strangers to whom we were aliens, Vicky and I treasured our familiarity. We were establishing a cozy Saturday morning routine that we interrupted only during a particularly loathsome cartoon sequence. With nothing missed, we used this time to get up out of our nest, go into the kitchen, pour cereal and milk into our bowls, and wait for our favorite shows while slurping through our breakfast on TV trays.

Then, looking up from our bowls at the sounds coming from the television set, Vicky and I would sing out, my voice soaring above hers, "HERE I come to save the DAY; that means Mighty Mouse is on his WAY!" There we sat until we heard our mother, exasperated, say, "Go get dressed right NOW. And turn off that TV!"

In Chile, I was outgoing and often in the company of friends and family. In this new environment, I turned inward. I became timid as an extraterrestrial might feel. TV opened me up. Its programs took me out of my changed reality and placed me where I could express, through fantasy, my buried, fun-loving character.

In time, my interest in cartoons receded and cowboy shows came to the fore. I best loved the evening ones: *Rawhide, Sugarfoot,* and *Have Gun Will Travel* were among my favorites. I wanted to be a cowboy. Gingham fabrics, cap guns in holsters, cowboy hats worn at an angle, cowboy boots. I wanted them all.

We couldn't afford to dress me in play costumes, no matter how many times I whined, "But Mommy . . ." However, I did get a roll of caps, a gingham bandana, a leather bolo tie, and a few other small cowboy accoutrements. Without a gun to fire my ammo, I'd pull off several caps from the roll, place them on the sidewalk, and hit them consecutively with a rock. The staccato bam-bam-bams added drama to my playacting. Not my sister, but my little brother, Jimmy, joined me in these games.

Vicky didn't share my love for the Wild West. She was growing into adolescence and puberty, and away from childhood fantasy worlds. The Danish recliner soon could not hold us both.

In Grandma's house an enclosed patio off the dining room had been converted as Vicky's and my bedroom. Grandma covered the concrete floor with a green shaggy rug and placed two twin beds perpendicular to each other against two walls. The room was large, larger than any room Vicky and I had shared before. Sliding glass doors opened to the outside patio, and a full-sized window looked out into the garden. In one corner of the room next to my bed was a tall, narrow, five-shelved triangular open cabinet. My grandmother called it the "whatnot." It held odds and ends and whatever trinkets needed a place to park. Once in my possession, it held my favorite items, ones I liked to display for my viewing pleasure. Most fun for me was to arrange a shelf in a stage-set manner.

During my cowboy phase, two of the whatnot shelves were dedicated to Western paraphernalia. There I displayed my rolls of caps, bandana, and bolo tie. A Western-dressed doll and figurines would sit on those shelves on occasion. When my mother got after me to clean up the room, I spent most of the time dusting and rearranging my shelves, with little time left for picking up the rest of the room.

As my sister and I grew into our own changed and distinctive lives, school friendships found me. I came out of the cowboy phase and out of being my brother's playmate. I discovered commonality with other girls in my class. My foreignness began to fade away. My lonely fantasies diminished.

At the start of the new school year, a girl from another school transferred into my class. She was not shy as I was, but independent, self-assured. And she wanted to be my friend. Soon enough, Sue and I became best friends. Together we created our own shared fantasy world, a world of girl secrets and made-up stories.

Television took a different turn for me. No longer did it provide me with a portrayal of an idealized, imagined self. It now lured me as it had upon first experiencing it: the intrigue of twists and turns in the stories and surprise endings. With Sue by my side, we ventured into the depths of fright with *The Twilight Zone, Alfred Hitchcock Presents,* and the like. *Perry Mason* tested our deductive reasoning. We howled together watching and remembering scenes from *I Love Lucy.* Gradually, I found that I was OK with where I had come to live, that I could find a place thousands of miles from the country I had left with such reluctance.

Because I Still Love Your Father

In early 1959, after we had settled in Sacramento, my mother took Vicky to see Dr. Gerbode, who had performed Vicky's 1957 surgery. He concluded that Vicky needed a second open-heart operation. He performed the surgery, and at the beginning of summer, my father arrived in California. Oh, joy! Our family, reunited.

At the time, we were living with Grandma Stevens, who had been sharing her upstairs bedroom with my mother. Now my father joined them. It was a large room, but still, it had to be awkward. There was no other bedroom. There must have been some way of carving out a private space in that room, but I didn't pay attention to such matters at that age, so I can't be sure of their sleeping arrangements.

Like a dreamer hoping for a miracle for so long that when it appears, she forgets how it came to be, I have no memory of my father's reunion with our family. He was there, and that was all I cared about. I can, however, conjure a likely scenario of his arrival:

My mother and grandmother drive the two hours from Sacramento to the San Francisco airport to pick up my father. We kids were told that we all wouldn't fit in Grandma's 1956 salmon-colored Ford. "And, his plane is scheduled to arrive long after your bedtime." "But Mommy," we wailed, "we want to go too!" "You'll see him soon enough, don't worry." A neighbor comes over to stay with us, and with all the excitement and anticipation over the last week, we are exhausted, and I fall asleep as soon as I climb into bed.

"Papo!" we all cry out early the next morning, running up the stairs to greet him. "Shh!" is my grandmother's answer, catching us before we can burst into the bedroom. "He's had a late night; your father is exhausted. Let him sleep a while." Reluctantly Vicky, Jimmy, and I walk back down the stairs, to breakfast and to watch our morning TV programs. Three-year-old Jimmy is off to play with his trucks. Vicky and I settle into our TV-watching chair, Grandma's Danish recliner. "Captain Sacto calling the control tower: tell all the boys and girls I'm coming in!" Just then I feel a large hand cover my eyes and a familiar voice say, "Guess who!" With one movement, Vicky and I turn around in the seat we share, "Papo!" There he stands and my mother beside him, just as they should be. Jimmy runs and tumbles in to greet the father he has been missing for six months.

I did not pay much attention to my mother and father's relationship; I only considered my own relationship to them, to us as a family, and I was happy. I yearned for our return to Chile but dared not look too far into the future. My siblings and I spent the hot, dry Sacramento summer days in the shade of Grandma's lemon tree, Vicky resting on a chaise lounge, Jimmy and I chasing each other around, running through the lawn sprinklers turned on as high as they would go. My mother and grandmother at their chores inside or taking a long break on the other chaise lounge, a thick book with tiny print, open-faced, resting on my mother's lap. "Mommy, you're going to lose your place!" I'd cry out. But she had already drifted off into sleep. My father spent his days looking for work. On warm evenings we'd set up a card table or two under the same redolent lemon tree. There, the six of us—my mother, my father, my grandmother, Vicky, Jimmy, and I—would have our dinner in the waning summer light, mosquitoes buzzing around us.

There were tensions: concern for my sister's full recovery, my father's job prospects, six of us living together in my grandmother's crowded home, the return to a school that barely welcomed Vicky and me. For my mother and father, another baby on the way.

The Sacramento area was known for its prolific summer tomato crop. Although my father had a degree in agronomy and a graduate degree in botany from UC Berkeley, he was unable to find work in his professional field. "The only job I was ever offered," my father told me years later, "was working in the fields, picking tomatoes." *What kind of bigoted country is this?* I thought, as I heard his words. But at the time, I held an empty box of explanations. At the end of the summer, my father left us and his pregnant wife to return to his own country. Eight months later my mother's water broke. Grandmother drove her to the hospital. The child, a boy, died in childbirth.

Edmundo's departure marked the end of my parents' life together. Were they aware of it then? Did they have hopes, did they promise each other that their love would endure and bring them together again, in one country or the other? My parents did not divorce then. And they did correspond, for a time. How exhilarating to receive those blue aerogram envelopes stuffed with onionskin blue paper with my father's indecipherable handwriting addressed to Celia Pisano at our various Sacramento homes! Some of those pages were for Vicky, Jimmy, and me.

The letters' frequency diminished over time. By the end of 1969, my parents divorced, when my father wished to remarry. He had been without a family for too long; loneliness had worn him down. Our family unit was broken and would never be made whole again.

When my father's attempt to establish a living in Sacramento failed, my mother altogether stopped talking about our Chilean family. I believed she had forgotten. Only much later, as my age approached hers when she died, would my conviction begin to crumble. I now believe that keeping silent was my resolute mother's attempt to protect us from grieving our losses. Even her favorite proverb, "If wishes were horses, then beggars would ride," she must have known would be too harsh for her children to bear.

But I could not forget so easily. I didn't even try to. I chose to wallow in and indulge my grief, secretly. I stood in the silence of the closet until the wave of sadness left me. Then I'd open the door to return to daily life as it had become. "Vivian," I'd hear my mother's voice from the kitchen, "where were you? It's time to set the table." At home, the home we left, I never had to do such chores. They were the maid's responsibility. Everything was different here.

My mind was full of questions: "When will we go home to Chile, to our family? Why is our father not with us? Mommy, you haven't talked to us; don't we matter?" And then, when it became obvious we were staying, "Why can't we go even for a visit?" Questions that I, unable to bear the weight of answers I was unprepared to hear, didn't ask. Questions that came with emotional barriers—not only mine but also my mother's and my sister's—prevented probing.

Vicky too was mum. I could not discuss my anguish with her. After all, Vicky was at the center of our US presence. She must have felt the weight of that responsibility.

These questions lived on inside me, and there they smoldered, turning to resentment toward my mother (she, after all, brought us and kept us here) and guilt (I should be thankful that my mother, single and alone, raised us and gave us the best she could). Resentment and guilt wove through the fabric of my bond to my mother.

But there were times when I, unable to see any solutions to my teenage troubles, gladly ceded decisions to her. In high school, after five years of acclimation and seemingly successful Americanization, I found myself again a target of taunts. This time, not because my difference was as a lone foreigner but, I believe, because my small circle of close friends and I were outside the popular culture of a cliquish school. We liked to do our own things, have our own fun, take risks. If boys from their crowd approached us, yes, we would go to the party. If these boys attempted to take advantage of us, we would repudiate their groping. Were they offended by rejection, by my saying "no" when they wanted "yes"? Did their evolving manhood feel wounded, their pride suffer? Did they think they could wear me down until I acceded?

I was too sensitive to their subsequent bullying and their lies. I knew I was not their only target; I knew they raised their status in their own group by demeaning others outside their circle. But the estrangement I had experienced upon coming to this country resurged. I was an alien, waking up on a morning to find toilet paper strewn all around our front yard and wound around its trees, seeing boys drive by our house on a Saturday night yelling obscenities, hearing mumbling and stares in the school hallways. My grades suffered. I lost all interest in school.

By my junior year, I wanted out of high school. I appealed to my mother. "I'm not going there—I can't stand it anymore!" She didn't disagree. Instead, she looked for other options, even those she could barely afford. I might not tolerate that school, but no child of hers would be a high school dropout.

"Enough," said my mother. "Next fall I'm enrolling you in the Catholic high school." An all-girls school near Sacramento State College, several miles from home, St. Francis had recently opened their new campus. I anticipated the grief from missing my friends, mostly my two best friends. I was shy and knew that making new friends would be difficult. In a Catholic all-girls school, I would be one of the few non-Catholic students. And because the school had no midterm program, I would need to repeat a semester. But I wanted out of McClatchy High. The prospect of removal from a toxic environment and my hope for a renewed interest in academics took precedence. I did not put up a fuss and ceded this decision to my mother. In this move to a foreign environment, however, I knew what I was getting into, and I accepted it with eyes open. We discussed the transition at length. It proved to be the right move. St. Francis renewed my confidence and interest in academic achievement. I thank my mother for her decision.

After thirteen married years in Chile, Celia, then forty years old, was on her own, emotionally and financially. While writing this memoir, I asked tía Sylvia for her recollections of my parents' break. In a letter to me she wrote, "Ed continued to send all his salary to the US, which was reduced by the exchange rate. It was a small amount, but it was all that he had." In those years, I was under the impression that my father did not send money, but perhaps he did. If he did, it was a meager amount that he could afford.

To make her own way and that of her three young children, my mother immersed herself in a career of teaching and study. She raised us with strong determination and a will to ensure that we received a good education. "You must go to college," she'd tell us. Your college degree can't be taken from you. With it, you can pursue a career. You don't need to depend on someone else to support you, especially when you're forced into self-reliance, such as was her mother and then she herself. Beauty, and its power to attract, has no lasting power, whereas an educated mind, she believed, endures.

Preserving beauty, however, was important to her. As she grew older, my mother tried to recapture her waning youth: makeup applied inexpertly; coloring that thinned and dried her soft, fine blond hair; dieting that robbed nutritional value; drink that promised to assuage but only heightened loneliness and disappointment and further compromised her physical aspect. Did she mourn her lost physical beauty in her later years, after years of drinking a nightly whiskey and soda by herself, years without my father, without a partner? As with her private feelings, her alcohol problems were not acknowledged and not to be mentioned. I became increasingly intolerant and critical of her behavior, her decline, and her attempts to regain the beauty that was slipping away.

I could see that an unsteady hand applied her lipstick. She lost the ability to paint inside the lines as a child is taught to do. Thickly penciled eyebrows arched above her green eyes, lost under a painted mask. "Mommy," I wanted to say but dared not, "let me help you." Instead, I looked away.

"I know you're not going to approve of what I did," my mother said a few years later. "I got a face lift." No, immersed in my own bloom of youth, I didn't approve. I took in her words but said nothing.

On a summer evening years later, as my mother and I were driving on Freeport Boulevard in Sacramento, I gathered my seventeen-year-old courage and, in the silence inside the car, turned to her: "Why haven't you divorced and found someone to marry?" She averted her eyes from the road, gripping the steering wheel to face me fully: "Maybe it's because I still love your father." We both remained silent the rest of the way to wherever we were going.

The nymph replies to the shepherd:

> *The flowers do fade, and wanton fields,*
> *To wayward winter reckoning yields,*
> *A honey tongue, a heart of gall,*
> *Is fancy's spring, but sorrow's fall.*[1]

---

1. "The Nymph's Reply to the Shepherd," attributed to Walter Raleigh.

And if not love, then what? What stirred inside that five-foot-one, well-formed frame of my mother that drove her to abandon her life as she knew it and start anew, in a country thousands of miles away in location, situation, tradition? I never asked her. I can't now. I'm free to make up my own stories. She's not here to either affirm or deny any of my speculations.

I posit it was a chance to get away—from family responsibilities she had taken on for so long. Away from the goodie-two-shoes reputation given to female eggheads like her. A way to air her own, little-known adventurous, spirit. For expectations are often placed on the eldest female sibling, especially in a family headed by a single, working mother. And more so when that family has been ingrained with the Protestant work ethic.

Celia fulfilled homemaker and caretaker roles at an early age. After her father died and her mother went to work, she looked after her sister, Helen, and her baby brother, Bob. Helen was the wild child, and Bob was the budding future electrical engineer, whom she'd find in his room fiddling with his self-built ham radio. Two disparate children required learning an effective parenting technique. In my mind's eye, I imagine Helen, half-dressed, without breakfast, running out the door to play with her friends. And Bob, rising early to deliver newspapers on his bike. Then, instead of returning home after his route, riding up to San Diego's Mount Helix with his ham radio where he'd find better reception to reach operators throughout the world. At least big sister saw that he had had a breakfast of sorts. The evidence was there: a half-eaten banana on the kitchen counter, the remnants of a bowl of cornflakes and milk in the sink, and soggy cornflakes on the table and floor.

Neither one bothered to pick up their clothes, make their beds, tidy their room before setting off on their day's activities. She wasn't going to clean up for them but would make them clean it up themselves. And, so that they would learn well, she'd leave her breakfast dishes for them to clean up as well. Badgering and demanding, I would say, was her technique. At least that was what she used with us, her own kids.

Celia learned how to cook and she learned well. Her cooking skills were well honed by the time she got to be my mother. Maybe her cooking expertise was spurred by her own mother's less-than-desirable conventional kitchen skills. Or, it could very well be that in seeking recipes that delightfully titillated unfamiliar taste buds, she expressed her proclivity for adventure.

Perhaps my mother's ties to her home and family weakened for lack of sufficient recognition or appreciation from her mother. Helen, the middle child, escaped her mother's disapproval by eloping. Of the remaining two, Celia and Bob, Bob received his mother's charm. I heard about and witnessed Grandma being smitten with her son. "See here," she'd point out among a gallery of family photos on her wall, "this is your Uncle Bob." Prominent at the center of the photos was her youngest, bent over a drafting table at the Jet Propulsion Laboratory, where he worked, with two companions looking on, examining his designs for communication systems for NASA space missions. Grandma didn't express such outward affection or particular appreciation for her eldest child.

After my parents separated, my mother never even dated anyone else. She socialized with other teachers and friends, mostly women and couples. I never saw any men come to our house to take her on a date. If she did date, she kept it hidden from us. Although once— and only once—I saw something I wasn't meant to see.

Mr. Alexander was our TV repairman. He had a large family; his older children attended the school that Vicky and I went to. One of the daughters was in Vicky's class; another was in mine, and a friend. I was fourteen or fifteen at the time. Mr. Alexander came by our house occasionally to fix our TV or dropped by to say hello when in the neighborhood to fix someone else's. His must have been a booming business, judging by the number of times he came to our neighborhood. "Vicky, did you see Mr. Alexander and mom?" It was past our bedtime; Vicky and I had been asleep. Something had awakened me. I realized that I was thirsty and got up to get a drink of water from the kitchen. As I opened the door from the hallway to the living room, I saw Mr. Alexander and my mother on the couch, its back to me, in a kissing embrace. I closed the door quietly and crept back to our bedroom.

"What about it?" my half-asleep sister answered. "He came over tonight after you went to sleep."

"Come with me. Take a peek."

By then, there was nothing to see. They were sitting across from each other, talking. "TV" and "television," I noted, were words missing from the bits of conversation we heard.

"But I swear, Vicky, I saw them kissing!"

Our TV continued to need servicing, and Mr. Alexander continued to come by to "take a look at it." I never witnessed another such scene, but I wouldn't rule out that it might have been repeated.

My mother was an attractive and intelligent woman. She enjoyed her social life, however limited it was—bridge parties, school events, family picnics. Most of her evenings were spent alone—often with an after-dinner glass of bourbon and water—grading her students' papers, reading, or studying for one or another class she was taking. She seldom watched TV in those days. "Television," she'd say, "numbs the mind." Whether men felt challenged by her intelligence and independence and baggage (a category I put myself and my siblings in) or she shunned potential partners, being too busy raising three children, working more hours than her teaching job required, and furthering her own education, she wouldn't say.

In the silence following her words—that she still loved my father—I glimpsed the depth of pain residing inside her. I realized then how I had misinterpreted the manifestations of her pain—angry outbursts, strict parental guidelines, evenings with whiskey, silence—as character flaws. In my late teens, I was still too young and too self-involved to understand and forgive. But her answer allowed me to peer into her character. In that moment I felt the empathy I know she deserved. "Mommy," I wish I'd said, "I understand you, and I miss him too."

Return

Ten years passed before I went back to Chile. By then, toward the end of 1968, I was twenty and had spent half my life in California. No excuses or justifications were needed for my first trip back to Chile. My mother, to my delighted surprise, needed no persuasion. She knew this was right for me. She encouraged me.

In preparation for my return, I took a few college Spanish classes. The language that had slipped away from me began to reemerge. "I just have a natural facility for languages," I would tell my teachers and fellow students when they, impressed, commented on my pronunciation. I was ashamed to reveal that I had lost my native language and to call attention to the foreignness that I had so effectively learned to hide.

As departure time neared, I tried to imagine what my return would feel like. I had no strategies to cope with the emotions surrounding this trip. Would the little girl of ten years earlier be recognizable in the young woman? What remained of the strong friendships my cousins and I had formed when we were together? Would my abuelita remember that she had told me I was her favorite among the cousins? I never forgot this declaration throughout the ten years we were apart. But I was not who I had been then. I was changed by my circumstances: different customs, my American friends, the emerging social consciousness of those times, my adolescence, and my assimilation into American society.

After a celebratory lunch near the San Francisco airport with family and a few friends, I boarded the Pan Am plane to arrive in Santiago nearly twenty-four hours later. Pan Am had been the airline that flew us to San Francisco ten years earlier. It was a long flight then, too, and filled with anxiousness for what I would find upon landing. Anxiety resurged on this return flight.

Memories of my first bumpy airplane flight to the States ran through my head. I thought about the complementary Butter Mints with which the stewardesses were so generous: a way of assuaging a sad child. I ate all they gave me until those Butter Mints retaliated. They brought on an airsickness much more acute than the sickness I often experienced on long car trips. I soon learned what those little sacks in the seat pockets were for, but not in time to contain my erupting stomach. Oh, I can imagine the stewardesses regretting their foolish nursing notions. I still cannot tolerate the taste and texture of those little soft candies as they dissolved in my mouth. My stomach still protests just by my thinking about Butter Mints.

This time, my Pan Am flight was uneventful and smooth, yet long and sleepless. I spent much of the twenty-four airborne hours in reflection.

In 1958 I had assumed that my trip to the US would be temporary. In 1968 I wondered if my trip to Chile would be only a visit or more than that, a return home. That old desire still remained and surfaced, occasionally.

But ten years from childhood to young adulthood can create estrangements, I thought, from those who appeared in my mind as I remembered them and from memories of that time sweetened by the passing years.

We had had little communication with our Chilean family once we came to the US. Occasional letters arrived from my father, far fewer from anyone else. Telephone calls hardly ever occurred and visits never. A cold turkey extraction left me with long-lasting withdrawal symptoms.

During the 1950s, the world was much less connected than it would be ten years later. Foreign travel and communication were expensive. Telephone communication was not just expensive; it was complicated. You would first call the long-distance operator (always a she) to provide information about the intended call: phone number, recipient, and who was making the call. You would hang up and wait while the operator proceeded to the next step, to contact her counterpart in the foreign country (also always a she) and relay the particulars of the intent to call. The foreign operator would then dial the number and announce that a long-distance call was being attempted by the stated party, from the stated country. The recipient would hang up while the two operators worked toward establishing the connection.

When (and if) successful, the local operator called you, and the foreign operator called the person you wanted to reach. You had to speak loudly over the static and hope for a sustained connection. Unreliable it was, hardly worth the effort to understand each other's "I miss you." Letters were the best option. We used the thinnest, most lightweight stationery to save on postage. And if you wrote on both sides of the paper, you had to make sure you wrote without a leaky pen and used light pressure on the paper. If you didn't write both "Air Mail" and "Correo Aéreo" clearly on the envelope, your letter would be traveling by boat for the next few months.

My father's letters to me began with "My dear guatita." *Guatita,* which translates, at best, as "little tummy," was one of his pet names for me. For I was a roly-poly girl; baby fat, I was told. "Monkey-face" was another of his pet names for me when I was a little girl. From six thousand miles away, I'd cry every time I opened one of his letters. Those loving yet mildly mocking nicknames, innocently intended to poke fun, to endear, were a way of telling me, instead of saying the real words, "I love you—you are my daughter."

I thought about memories he would have of me and how they could influence how he would see me as an adult. I imagined that he remembered me as a sweet and innocent child. A little monkey uninitiated to life's hazards who loved to explore, take risks, climb trees, and jump down to the ground. To feel what it was like to parachute down from the branch, I once popped open a large black umbrella and leaped, just like Mary Poppins. A scientific experiment, one might say, with the evidence ultimately disproving my theory. I don't remember this incident at all; I live the memory only through my mother's telling. Lucky for me, I didn't sustain damages other than the loss of its recollection.

I recalled other childhood pranks, such as when I slid my five-year-old head through the railing of a second-story deck at my grandparents' house. I suppose this was another scientific experiment. If my head slips in through the two vertical bars so easily, I deduced, I can likewise bring it back with just as much ease. I didn't count on the panic that the first unsuccessful try prompted. Once on the other side of the railing, my head felt itself doubling in size. And from that point on, nothing worked. No twisting right and left, no movement sideways and up. My head was stuck, and I would be there until the bars were sawed off. I yelled for help, and when others came to see what was the matter, they were quite amused to find such a comical, entertaining sight. But I wouldn't do with jokes at this time; it wasn't fair. With slow and patient instruction from one of the adults—my father?—I wriggled free.

How much had these and other shenanigans formed my father's view of me? And how much of who I was for the first ten years of my life stayed with him after I left? I was a young woman, on my return trip, who had outgrown baby fat, mischievousness, and innocence.

Less curious and adventurous in the ways of a child, but still interested in and exploring life's offerings.

Upon our arrival in San Francisco in 1958, my American grandmother was waiting for us, arms akimbo, a stranger to me, ready to drive us to Sacramento to her home. Arriving in Santiago in 1968, I trembled with anxiety as I walked down the stairs of the plane to the tarmac, looking around for something and someone familiar. There he was, my father in the crowd of people, waiting for me. His dress was sober: dark-colored, loose jacket and pants, nondescript shirt. I recognized him immediately by his eyebrows, two straight horizontal lines ending with long, tail feather hairs extending nearly beyond his face. His hair was thinner, with strands of gray weaving through. I had remembered a tall, towering man, but ten years later he looked to be of average height. Neither of us could run up to each other in a sudden embrace. We were both too shy; it had been too long. Nevertheless, there were tears in our eyes in that awkward moment. We picked up my bags and drove to my father's apartment in central Santiago in his Buick (pronounced "Bweeck" in Chilean Spanish).

How much of the child remained in my father's view of me? Probably not much. But I wished it so, having been severed from him—wanting my family, as it had been then, sewn back together again. Even so, for those weeks I was with him, every so often he would approach me with the same look I recollected when he called me *"guatita"* and "little monkey" but just short of those words and the words behind them. I could see in his eyes the sad look of missed time. I was and was not his daughter. I had been his child, but formative years passed without his influence or parenting. Now it was time for the grown daughter and the older father to forge new images of each other and a renewed parent-child relationship.

Two Worlds

I looked to return to a world that had lived ten years in my memory, just as I had left it when a ten-year-old child. But I found myself an outsider in an unfamiliar environment. In those ten years, Chile had changed for me, and I for it. Like me, my cousins were now young adults. Although our early bonds endured, our different socialization experiences divided us. I grew up in the 1960s United States, amid much social and political turmoil. The '60s generation in the US belonged to the youth, our voices loosening social mores, questioning authority, protesting involvement in the Vietnam War, and expressing freedom from parental and sexual controls.

Chile, in contrast, had experienced a period of relative stability. Tradition still reigned; the young still succumbed to established mores and expectations. Families remained a focus for social activities; Catholicism held its sway. Among the middle and upper classes, proper social conduct was expected and, for the most part, followed. People placed high value in maintaining civility and smooth relations in social situations, even if, in more intimate settings, they felt and expressed contrary sentiments. In the US, I had become accustomed to open, revelatory social interactions. If you didn't like someone, you didn't talk to them. Or if you did, you didn't pretend to like them.

My large family drew me into a whirlwind of lunches and elaborate afternoon teas. What a stark contrast to our small family Sunday dinners in Sacramento with just my mother, grandmother, sister, and brother. Ten years of absence melted away when my father, beloved abuelita, nono, cousins, and aunts and uncles welcomed me.

But I soon realized that I was an alien there too. I had become a gringa, with gringa values and mores. I felt merely a visitor, a traveler with rusty language skills. My Chilean family embraced me. But, now a stranger, I could no longer gauge the balance between expressions of familial bond and the cordiality that Chileans give their guests.

"Talk slower," my aunts would implore their children, "so that Vivian can follow what you're saying." But Chileans are social and talkative and speak rapidly so as to insert their words into a conversation. They seem the roadrunners of Spanish speakers.

My father or another English-speaking relative would attempt to translate for me: "What your uncle said, Vivian, was that . . ."

By then, the conversation around us had turned to other subjects. No way could I keep up with the flow. So I struggled on, picking phrases out of the milieu of voices and contributing to conversations in a slower, abbreviated version of my native language.

One evening, I went to a party with my cousins, the first without aunts and uncles and chaperones. Just some cousins and their friends; my peers, in their twenties. I met a boy there. He was so cute, and he was attracted to me. We danced, we talked, we made a date. We all danced long into the night. I was having fun.

On the day of our appointed date, I took time in preparations: washing and arranging my hair in that special way I had learned from my American friends—wrapping my long wet hair around my head until it dried and fell in soft waves on my shoulders—trying on different outfits, applying some but not too much makeup.

Thoughts of love ran through my head: *We will fall in love with each other. He will plead for me to give up my American life, stay in Chile. Maybe even get married? I will, yes, I would stay.*

Didn't my mother give up her American life for her love? She, after all, gave up the country of her birth to live in a culture foreign to her—in Chile, where her young husband beckoned her. But I, on the contrary, would be returning to my natal country.

This gringa will revert to the chilena *she was born to be,* I said to myself.

The hour came. My father and I sat in the living room, he playing solitaire and I waiting. A half hour passed, no date.

Chilean time? No; Chileans are punctual.

An hour passed. I went to my room, changed my clothes, then sought solace with my father. I told him about how much fun I had at the party and about the boy, the one who made a date with me. "He looked like he had fun too."

My father listened, put his arm around me. "Vivian," he said with a compassionate voice, "once a Chilean boy has a commitment for a date, he doesn't take kindly to the girl's flirting with other boys. That may be acceptable in the US, but not here."

Oh no, I thought. I shouldn't have danced with those other boys. I realized then, I am a cultural foreigner here. It's not just the language.

I thought about my parents and their cultural divide. The indelible force of love lured them together, convincing them that they could surpass all obstacles in a life together no matter how disparate their backgrounds. The home they would build together would result in a synchronous blending of two worlds. Is that what they imagined as they basked in their romance? But love could not withstand the force of their cultural differences. They couldn't have imagined in the beginning that their union would end in disappointment and regret, with some bitterness—and that their failed love would continue to influence their lives as well as the lives of their children.

For all those years from the time we left Chile until my own adulthood, I could not, or would not, acknowledge the sadness that my mother must have felt from the breakup of our family and the disappointment she must have felt over her failed thirteen-year attempt to live so far away from the world she had been rooted to. Instead, I blamed her for uprooting us. Only after my mother's death would I come to realize that she may have felt resentful too: bringing up three young children on her own, with little financial help from her faraway husband. It had to be difficult for her. Nevertheless, she shielded me from feeling her pain. And I became the ungrateful daughter.

I have no direct experience of the way in which the loss of love influenced my father. I hardly knew him once we moved away, and then only through occasional correspondence. Letters from an absent father to his daughter can be carefully planned and worded, whereas an ever-present mother cannot conceal emotions underlying her spoken words, even when that daughter ignores or misinterprets them.

My father fell into a period of financial difficulty while developing what was later to become a prominent scientific career. And throughout much of that time, neither Chilean pesos valued well against the US dollar, nor were scientists and professors sufficiently compensated. We lived solely on my mother's meager teacher's salary.

My mother never spoke ill of my father. In fact, she rarely mentioned him or our life in Chile at all. I did not then see this as a sign of pain; I saw it as a dismissal, a voiding. I placed the responsibility for our emigration on her. Perhaps my own attitude deepened her pain. I didn't see it then; I, too, felt pain.

And my father? Since my formative years were spent without him, he became part of my memories of an idealized life left behind, the stuff of my longing. As an adult, I saw my father only on widely separated visits. On those visits, we treasured the little time we had together, knowing that we would soon enough be apart again.

Even so, I never felt bitterness overtake him. On occasion, I saw an underlying melancholy, which I attributed to loss, a love for my mother, and so too, love for his children and regret that he could not be with us. His letters to my siblings and me were full of yearning to be with us again. Letters that were filled with information about his life in botany; news of our extended family; and thoughts about social, political, and economic forces playing out in Chile always ended with a longing to be together again. Unlike my feelings toward my mother, I placed no blame on him for our family's fate.

On one of my visits to Chile, my abuelita spoke of my father's sadness: how this man, brokenhearted by the separation from his family, and further distressed by his inability to provide financial support across the distance that separated us from him, turned to a lonely life. "He suffered much when your mami left with you, his children," she said. He bought a parcel of land in the remote area of the island across the Strait of Magellan, Tierra del Fuego. Sheep grazing was the only industry in this vast, windswept, and cold frontier. There he lived for a year or two in a tiny shack, grazing sheep for wool. I still have some small, black-and-white photos of that shack on a vast, bare plain covered with snow.

But sheep farming was not a life he could sustain for long without involving his true calling and career as a botanist. So the little house and parcel of grazing land with sheep-shearing facilities became a summer retreat where he'd go to fish and relax from his scientific pursuits. He rented his land and sold his sheep to his neighbor and made a home in the town where he was born, across the Strait of Magellan on the southernmost tip of the continent, Punta Arenas.

There he lived, established distinction in his field, remarried, weathered the various social and political upheavals in the latter quarter of Chile's twentieth century, and willed his parcel of land to his children, my siblings and me.

My mother, meanwhile, persevered and gained strength and resolve. She furthered her education, established noteworthiness in her teaching career, and took pride in the three children she raised. She did not remarry. She never fully lost the underlying love she felt for the Chilean man she had fallen for so many years before.

Of the two, my mother had the greater emotional challenge. She crossed a cultural divide in her mid-twenties and sincerely attempted to, and in many ways successfully did, overcome intractable differences. But circumstances—my sister's health, financial difficulties—dictated another course of events that neither my mother nor my father had chosen or foreseen. No one could have known then how their relationship would end.

Lonely Propositions

Many years would pass before I understood the depth of my mother's loss. Yes, there were indications, pieces of conversation, emotional inflections in her voice, that I, in my youthful self-absorption, could not appreciate. Life experience and empathy would teach me otherwise. Only then could I open my mind and my heart to look back and recognize clues to her inner life.

On a 2005 visit to Chile, my then-ninety-two-year-old tía Sylvia recounted the time she and my uncle visited us in our Sacramento home about five or six years after we had left Chile. Sylvia said she was astounded to see the gallery of photographs in the hallway. "All of your mami's time in Chile with your father was prominent in most of her photographs. I realized then that she was still very much in love with Ed."

During my time growing up in Sacramento, I saw my mother as a harsh taskmaster, a rule-bound parent who displayed her devotion to her children by being strict, avoiding indulgence, and hiding emotions. I knew she loved us, but I wanted to be indulged and I wanted to share intimacies. Yet I could not tell her. I was afraid she'd reject my neediness.

I knew nothing of her intimate desires and aspirations. Instead, I saw her immersion in and dedication to teaching and education. Without a doubt, she expected us—Vicky, Vivian, and Jimmy—to receive a university education. College, she assured us, was not a place for girls to find their mates, nor to prepare for marriage. College was for becoming an educated citizen, for excelling as a human being. As both a teacher and mother, she promoted education as a means for self-development, transformation, and improvement. Preparation for college success meant that high school homework came before any leisure activities. "Vivian," I would often hear, "you cannot go to [fill in the blank] until you finish your homework. All of it." No further questions.

I seldom asked her to help me with homework. I could never ask her a simple yes or no question without receiving a long explanatory answer. I should have known to hold my question when I was eager to get my homework over with and move on. For the next fifteen minutes I'd be trapped in a lesson, which, under more leisurely circumstances—or with a more mature mind—I would have welcomed. Instead, my mind reeled with impatience; my body slowly backed away. After my fifteen minutes of fidgeting, I had forgotten both my simple question and her long-winded answer.

Slips in English grammar she did not easily tolerate. I could be on the phone talking to a friend, lax in my conversational speech, when I'd hear from across the room, "I'm going to *lie* down, not *lay* down!" "OK, OK," would be my exasperated retort. Or my answer would be the silence of disregard, or, if particularly feisty, I'd ensure that she heard me utter some popular youthful jargon I knew she couldn't bear to hear—"Cool, man, that's tough!"

Some of her lessons, however, stuck. Certain grammatical errors jar my adult self. I can hardly get through reading a passage where "who" is used for "whom" without retreating and reconstructing the sentence in my mind to its grammatical accuracy. And when I hear someone start a sentence with "Me and her," I lose concentration, and subsequently comprehension of and interest in the words that follow. Thanks, Mom.

My mother loved teaching. She taught junior high and high school Spanish-language classes from the time we arrived in the US until she retired in 1986. She did her job well. Accolades for her teaching skills came from her superiors and colleagues as well as her students. "You are Mrs. Pisano's daughter?" a former student exclaimed when I first met him long after high school. "Your mother was the best teacher I ever had. Difficult, yes, but sincerely interested in teaching her students Spanish." A difficult, demanding mother too, I agreed in silence.

During periods of heavy workload, my mother recruited Vicky and me to help her grade papers. She assigned us the multiple-choice tests. That was the easy part. My mother had the more difficult and time-consuming task of grading the essay questions.

In spite of our help, teaching, for her, was a full-time endeavor. Up early; prepare lunches for my sister, brother, and me; and out of the house by 7:30 a.m. to be ready for classes at 8:00 a.m. She had a class for every period of the school day except for one free period, available for meeting with students, preparing lessons, and keeping up with professional journals. School days ended at 3:15, and unless she needed to stay to supervise a student's after-school detention, the formal teaching day was done. But the workday didn't end there. Before heading home, there'd be after-school errands to the grocery store, the dry cleaners, the hardware store, and any number of other tasks a single mother must take care of. Best of all, she liked the more leisurely days, spending an hour or so with fellow teachers at their house or ours for shop talk.

Dinner preparations came next. Celia cooked no simple dinners. We ate gourmet meals from scratch with all the recommended food groups for growing kids. After dinner was her time to put up her feet and relax. We kids handled the cleanup, and my mother, with a whiskey and water on ice, sat down to attend to her students' papers.

I picture her sitting on the couch in her bathrobe, her feet up on the coffee table, one pile of papers next to her on the couch, another on the coffee table, her red pencil in hand studying, assessing each word. And next to her on the table, under the lamp, the ever-present glass. A textured glass with a bulge around the middle—a design, I suppose, to improve hand grip ability. The glasses came in a set of several colors, and I liked to see how each color transformed when filled with ice, whiskey and water. She'd take a sip every now and then, sips that would last until the last paper was graded, long after my bedtime.

During that time, those whiskeys never led to perceived inebriation. That came later, after I had moved away. I wonder if plunging into her work or clouding her mind helped her bury lonely, painful feelings and remembrances of a love she would never regain.

"Poor Celia," tía Sylvia lamented years later, "can you imagine any affection she would have felt for Chile? I felt so badly for your mother. I didn't blame her for not wanting to return to Chile after she left. But your father was also lonely for many years. He was all alone. He missed his family and felt isolated from the three of you, his children. Everyone with family . . . and your father, well, he was so alone. We felt so bad for him." She echoed Abuelita's concern for her son's loneliness.

Tía Sylvia's words take me back to the time a few years after my mother and the three of us left for the US when my father bought the land on that large, isolated, underpopulated, and inhospitable island across the Strait of Magellan from the tip of South America, Tierra del Fuego. Cold, windy, treeless, flat, uninviting for anything but grazing sheep. A lonely proposition.

In the early 1960s, government-owned land on the western, Chilean side of the island was subdivided and available for sale to private parties. Potential buyers were required to complete an application process and, if approved, would be eligible to purchase a large piece of land, albeit good for nothing except sheep grazing, for very little money. My father was among the fortunate who were accepted. He acquired ten thousand acres in two parcels, one for sheep to graze during the spring and summer and the other for their winter grazing. The spring-summer parcel was the more hospitable of the two, with low-lying hills and gentle valleys that cut the wind's fierceness. A deep, narrow river ran across the far end of the property. Near the entrance, my father constructed a tiny prefabricated house. It sat alone on a wide expanse of land. He spent most of the first year after his purchase living in it.

My father sent me pictures of his little house that first winter—covered with a thin layer of snow amid a vast emptiness I had never seen before. I imagined him sequestered there, all alone, writing, reading, playing solitaire with a well-worn deck of cards. What else does one do when there are no close neighbors to visit with, no inviting climate to greet an eager outdoors man? Only vast open spaces.

That small house provided scant comforts. No electricity, no telephone. Way off the grid. I suppose one can learn to savor canned and packaged foods when no refrigeration is available.

I imagine my father's evenings inside that little hut in front of the wood-burning stove, pouring himself a small glass of whiskey, lighting his cigarette, and settling back to read scientific papers and texts. When he looks up, is it at some sound he hears in the distance? Surely not children playing or dishes rattling in the kitchen or a sewing machine whirring in another room. No telephone to sound its ring. Perhaps he hears a condor's squawk as it flies overhead or the bleat of a lost sheep. There is nothing to see out the small window other than pitch-black night. No friendly faces come to share the warmth inside and engage in long conversations.

A scientific mind such as my father's cannot imagine apparitions or hear otherworldly sounds. No, his was a reasoned, no-nonsense mind. But his mind couldn't have been able to hold back sudden flights of loneliness, although I cannot picture what direction that loneliness took or how it played out in a scientific mind. Does such a mind rationalize and explain intimate feelings? Does it imagine scenarios that could have been? Does it pine for love lost? How did the loneliness that tía Sylvia alluded to manifest itself in my father's mind?

My father didn't make his home on that lonely, inhospitable island for long. He loved this terrain and the diversity he found in its monotonous immensity: the constantly changing weather; the surging clouds moving across the sky; the winding river; the wide-open spaces; the luscious, variegated botanical world living in miniature, protected from the harsh elements and visible only to the resolute and faithful botanist.

Although the land called to him, my father was not a sheep farmer. He was a scientist, a botanist eager to return to practice his profession. He sold his sheep, rented his two parcels to his neighbor, and returned to Punta Arenas across the Strait on the southernmost tip of the mainland to become one of the founders, in 1969, of the Instituto de la Patagonia, an institute devoted to the knowledge, development, and dissemination of the human and natural sciences of the area. His holidays, however, were spent fishing in the river running through his summer parcel on Tierra del Fuego.

Perhaps loneliness etches itself on a face. It carves wedges and pulls edges down. It tells of a deeply embedded need and longing lying within. I can see its evidence in photographs I have, even after his time of loneliness, after he had remarried and acquired another family. Whether his face expressed cheerfulness—joking, poking fun, telling stories—or seriousness—deep in thought resolving a problem, working on a crossword, studying a text, playing solitaire—the etchings, once inscribed, remained.

Many years later, after he remarried, after the Institute was well established and he was deep into his career, my father's wife Carmen wrote these words to me, here translated into English:

> Edmundo has suffered a lot, both economic problems and those of affect. That is, having lost you all was a very hard hit for him in addition to his economic situation that was unparalleled. I know that you all have also had your part of suffering, but you are young and still have the world in front of you.
>
> Ultimately your father has normalized, he has work he likes, where he is becoming well known and where he has a salary that, although not splendid, permits him to live normally. Also, he has a home; that is especially important for a human being. I have tried to give him much love to compensate in part for all the years of solitude he endured. Also, my children love him a lot, but you should understand that he will always feel the sadness of having you all so far away. He is in his best intellectual stage, but who can predict the number of years he will live! I hope there are many that he has in front of him, but only God knows.

I never had the opportunity to go to his land during my few and short visits to Chile while he was alive. The first time, the weather was too inclement; another time, his Russian Lada broke down. But years after his death, in 2005, I crossed the Strait of Magellan from the mainland to see the land that I had now inherited. Emotion and awe hit me upon entering the property.

The little prefabricated corrugated tin house, painted yellow, sits in the middle of this vast, flat, windswept piece of land at the end of the Earth. The sheep have been shorn and moved somewhere else to graze. Except for the yellow house and the sheep-shearing building beyond with its bales of wool ready to be shipped, nothing meets the eye but a springtime-green deserted pasture sprinkled with brilliant yellow dandelions.

Surrounding the house is a thigh-high white picket fence. I don't understand its purpose; do sheep wander in and around? Or is it an attempt to mask this harsh, desolate place and evoke a peaceful suburban life with family and children? A water tank sits on the roof.

I walk through the gate onto steps of cut logs leading to the door. Inside, I see simple, modest furniture: a bookcase with some tattered books for those lonely nights; a rusting old-fashioned stove; a couch that sags almost to the floor. The floor—I have to look twice to believe it—is covered with simulated-wood contact paper, buckling up here and there. Thin red gingham curtains adorn the kitchen windows. I wander into the bedroom: two tiny twin beds, in parallel position. But how can either bed hold a five-foot-eleven man? The closet door is open, and in the dark hangs the brown winter coat of its now-long-gone owner, my father. His initials, EP, are embroidered on the inside collar. The air is so still, there is no sound—at least none that I can hear, except the sound of my heart, beating with life.

In 2014, I revisited the land. The little yellow house stood just as it was nine years earlier. Nothing had changed: the contact-paper floor with the same buckling, the same books on the shelves, the red gingham curtains still hanging cheerfully on the windows. Only the closet was missing the brown winter coat. That coat is with me now, in my home in Berkeley, California.

Undutiful Daughter

As I left childhood and entered my teens, my resentment toward my mother grew. My mother, I was convinced, refused to acknowledge my pain; she intended for me to follow the path she had chosen for me without considering my wishes. Even though I didn't know what I wanted for myself, I knew I wanted to reject her plans for me. My mother separated me from my world, and I needed to separate from her.

Outwardly my reproach expressed itself as a contemptuous attitude. No thanks did she receive from me for driving my girl-friends and me to the movies, bowling, and parties—nor when, late at night, she drove back to pick us up. I was embarrassed to have my friends see my mother in a bathrobe and slippers. At least she didn't get out of the car for everyone else to see. And shame on me that time she drove me to that school party. I did not want her to come inside to greet the kids she knew from classes she taught at my school. I didn't even want her to accompany me to the door. She just drove off, disappearing in the distance while the hurt I had seen in her eyes remained in my vision. When the party was over, there she was, right on time, inside the car in her bathrobe and slippers to pick me up.

All those wild and crazy things I did—sneaking out of the house after everyone was asleep, attending parties my mother would not approve of—just to be different from her, to separate myself and show her: I'm not like you; you don't know who I am.

But I, the undutiful daughter, still felt hurt and shame when my mother called me on something I shouldn't have done; that she knew I would do such a thing, that I probably did it all the time, was unfair. What was that silly thing I had done—cut school? When I got caught, she asked, "Well, what did you do all day long?" "Nothing, Mom. Sue came over and we just watched TV." "Watched TV! You could have at least cleaned house if you were home all day!"

Decades later, I still could not be the dutiful daughter when she became sick at the end of her life. Vicky fulfilled that role, while I had the excuse of living one hundred miles away. When I came to see her for a few hours, I did so as a visitor.

Better to have approached her early on and directly, to have exposed my pain to her. We could have helped each other heal from our Chilean losses. She, having lost her husband to a country in which she had tried but could not assimilate, harbored a hurt much like mine. I wanted only to go back to Chile, to return to the comfort of my nest. My mother wanted to have our father join us, to make our nest whole in the comfort of her home country.

"You're just going to have to get used to doing what you don't want to do!" my mother told fifteen-year-old me. Another time, she said with an astonished look, "Bored? I don't even know what that means. I've never had the luxury of being bored. If you're bored, you can wash and wax the kitchen floor." These were my mother's attempts to teach her lazy daughter the value of work.

Summertime: no school, too hot to go outside, too tired to fight off this wave of sluggishness. It's only morning, and a long day stretches ahead to nowhere. I don't want to get up and get dressed. I don't have anything to wear for such an oppressive day. My white cotton sleeveless blouse has sweat stains from yesterday; my Bermuda shorts don't fit me well—they exaggerate my knock knees; and my legs are distastefully unshaven.

Besides, I like my bright-colored cotton pajamas, their tented top with stripes of reds, blues, and greens outlined by thin lines of gold filigree and loose, deep-blue bloomer bottoms. They make me happy. I don't like sleeveless white blouses; my bra shows through the armholes. I don't like pants that cut my crotch; I constantly have to adjust them when nobody's looking. It's too hot and sticky to tug and pull my clothes away from my body. I don't want to get up, I'm bored, I don't care what my mother says about boredom and luxury. And I for sure don't want to do housework. I think I'll just lie here in my cool pajamas until I hear her voice reach that edge between telling me what to do and making me do it: "Vivian, for the last time, get up!"

Why do I have to do things I don't want to do? What's wrong with lying around, having breakfast in bed, watching a little TV, taking a nap? I don't think I'd be happier or a better, wiser person doing things I don't want to do. I should tell my mother that I'd be a more pleasant daughter if I did things I wanted to do, when I wanted to do them. And that sometimes I just want to sit here and do nothing. Yes, I should tell her. But I don't. She's my mother. "Get to work!" she tells me. "Why?" my whiny voice asks. "Because I'm your mother, and I said so."

Take going to church, for example. At fifteen years old, I want to sleep in on Sundays. Especially when I stay up Saturday nights and go to the movies or bowling or just hang out with my girlfriends. I need my sleep. Instead, I have to get up early, iron my dress, polish my shoes—or at the very least, wipe off the scuffmarks with a soft rag— wash my face with cold tap water, and leave enough time to put on my makeup. All this just to go do something I don't want to do.

Church is boring. Sunday school is somewhat better. That's where Vicky and I usually go. My mother hands us each a couple of quarters for the tithe. Vicky and I enter the door to Sunday school while my mother and little brother head for the church doors.

Once, when I felt brave, I skipped Sunday school. First, I made sure I saw my mom go through the church doors. Then, standing outside the door to the Sunday school and with no one looking (other than my sister, whom I'd sworn to secrecy), I slipped away. Sue and I had arranged to meet at Winchell's Donuts. "If I'm not there by 11:00, then I couldn't get away," I had told her. No problem for her: Sue and her family would've gone to an earlier service at the Presbyterian church they attended. My tithe allowance was just enough for a Coke and a maple doughnut—no, better yet, a maple bar. I ran the few blocks to Winchell's, looked through the window, and saw Sue inside, waiting for me at the booth across the way. She didn't see me. A sudden wave of guilt overwhelmed me, and my hand shook as I wrapped it around the door handle. Push it open or run back to church? I could get back before the Sunday school's program was too far underway. I could tell the minister I had to use the ladies' room . . . Whoosh went the glass door as I pushed it open. Sue turned around, saw me, and smiled.

Lucky for me, my mother never (as far as I know) checked up on my Sunday school attendance.

When our Sunday school teacher was absent, Vicky and I had to accompany our mother and Jimmy for the church service. It happened every time: as soon as I would enter the quiet, stifling interior, a stupor came over me. Some hymn singing would perk up my tired body for a moment. Until the sermon. I could barely keep my eyes open. Eyes so heavy, I tried, tried to keep them open, but they overwhelmed my will. *Why am I here? I can't concentrate on a word the minister is saying*, my groggy mind whispered. Then and there I vowed to tell my mother—the next Sunday—that I wouldn't be going to church. Maybe I'd have the nerve by then. I'd rest my eyes for just one minute, then I'd pay full attention to the rest of whatever the minister was talking about. My brother jabbed his elbow in my side. I woke, gasping; the sermon was over. I looked over at my mother, whose gaze had just turned from me to straight ahead.

Boredom, stealthy pleasure, guilt, duty, and remorse all jumped around my mind, colliding, and confusing me.

My mother was clear about her priorities for me. Boredom was not one of them. Far from it. If I wanted to sleep over at my best friend's house on a Friday night, I had to be home early the next morning: "No later than 8:00 a.m.," my mother would tell me, to dust and vacuum the house. "Vicky shouldn't have to do your Saturday chores too."

No thoughts of tomorrow's obligations could stop Sue and me from staying up late—why waste away the time sleeping when we could watch the weird and strange on Friday night TV: Rod Serling's *Twilight Zone*, Boris Karloff's *Thriller*? Make a batch of chocolate chip cookie dough and eat half of it—the half with the most chocolate chips—raw? Riveted to the TV, with hearty screams of fright escaping from our mouths, unannounced: how could we sleep then? Nevertheless, I had to be home on Saturday by 8:00 a.m. Saturday morning at 7:30 a.m., I'd turn off the alarm the moment it rang. Quietly I would dress so as to avoid waking Sue up too, make up the twin bed, tiptoe through the room, gently unlock the kitchen door, and head home.

Once outside, I walked along the quiet, sleeping streets, listening to the birds and an occasional car moving toward its own obligatory destination, and I revived, fully awake. Those early weekend mornings were the best times to walk the streets, before the shopkeepers and markets opened, before exhaust from buses filled the atmosphere, and after the predawn sprinkling of newly mown lawns. The air smelled fresh and clean and earthy. Such a good time to let my mind wander, think about the day, figure out what I should have said to the girl in gym class who made fun of my purple-veined thighs, plan what I could say if I ran into the cute new guy in my homeroom class. And so, too, I would plot how to avoid doing the next thing I didn't want to do. "Mom, I'm not going to! I don't want to!" Ha!, I thought, I can never tell her that. And I never did.

My insensitive youthful behavior feels so shameful now. Is the relationship I had with my mother defined by the weight of my shame? Is there room in our relationship for that other me? The one who, when awakened alone in the night by a vivid, fearful dream, cried out, "Mommy!" But she's no longer there to comfort me or call out from the next room, "Go back to sleep, Vivian. Everything is all right—I'm right here."

"Do you know what your brother said to me?" my mother spits out. "Do you know what Jim accused me of?" I've just arrived from my home in the San Francisco Bay Area to spend the day with my mother in Sacramento. This is how she greets me as I enter her house. How long have these words been stirring inside, building and gaining momentum to explode with such force? "He said I have a problem! He said, 'Mom, you have a problem, you need help.' Well, he's the one who has problems." The problem Jim accused her of, she doesn't name. And from me, silence.

I was not brave enough then, in my late twenties, just codependent. I could have answered her. I could have said, "Mom, we know you have a drinking problem—you need to admit it." I could have asked her, "Why don't you seek help?" But her anger at Jim frightened me just as it did when, at a younger age, I felt terrified whenever I got in some trouble and had to face her. I could have said something. Instead, I trembled, unable to speak. Afraid of the consequences. Better not to say anything at all. Easier that way. Like mother, like daughter.

I wanted answers, but I could not ask the questions. I wasn't invited into her personal realm. I wasn't barred either. It was a fact understood. My mother taught me to respect my elders, who were entitled to have lives separate from prying children. But I should have seen another motive for her silence: she wanted to protect us from her grief.

Instead, I blamed her for her privacy. Why couldn't we, as a family, discuss what churned inside each one of us? And our mother, the person to whom we were most intimately related, distanced us from her emotional depths. I never saw her crying except those few times near the end of her life when she was compromised by a stroke.

Anger I did see. And I saw my father's too, when we lived together as a family. After bedtime, trying to fall asleep, from my bedroom upstairs I could hear my parents' voices in the living room down below growing louder and more penetrating. I strained but could not hear clearly; I couldn't shape the story of their argument. "Jesus Christ! What will you . . . ?" and "Not a damn thing!"

What did they argue about? Did they realize that my sister and I, frozen in our beds, could hear? Did they care?

"It's not fair. I want to know," I'd say. "She's too young to understand," adults around me would say. I say children are never too young to understand that there is something awry in their environment. They may not articulate what they feel or what they see, but they deserve answers to their questions. As for me, I felt I wasn't given the chance to learn, to digest, to form my own opinions about that which I was not told.

Fragments of phrases were hurled about. But not for long. I'd wait for their voices to subside into soft whispers. Relieved, I'd bask in the wake of the passing storm and fall into sleep.

When I was in my late teens, my mother said to me in a rare self-revelatory mood, "You can only hate someone you love deeply." After a beat, she added, "The best part of an argument is the making up, the sweetness that follows the argument." I imagined then what the child me could not: tender, endearing lovemaking.

I could never confront my mother's drinking. I didn't even try. Drink did not impair her behavior then, while my sister and I lived at home. But even if it had, I didn't talk about it. Taboo areas of family life I so wanted to break through, yet, unwittingly, I succumbed to them. My brother, Jim, seven years younger than I, grew up with a mother who was by then yielding to alcohol's sickness. Coming home on an evening, Jim might find a glass of whiskey and water spilled, the carpet stained, our mother passed out. Lift up dead weight, carry Mom to her room, put her to bed. And not a word said the next morning at breakfast.

Until he broke the taboo.

Siblings

Vicky and Jim—I wonder how they adjusted to life in the States. When we left Chile, Jimmy was only three, a little tyke with fine blond hair, wriggly energy, and a baby face. His American military-style crew cut did not, in my opinion, suit him, and neither did it toughen him. My heart melts when I look at pictures of my then-three-year-old brother. I see a vulnerable, frustrated soul living among a household of females: my mother, grandmother, sister, and me.

Jimmy missed the father he hardly knew. He held an emptiness that stayed with him throughout his life. Growing up, he had no male role model to look up to or to learn from. In our earliest days in Sacramento until he started school, he was cut off from male companionship—we had no male cousins in close proximity, nor any kids in our new neighborhood. So Jimmy was left to the play games directed by his older sisters: dressing up, playing house, playacting.

Seven years ahead of him, I liked to tease my little brother, gently and not, I believed, maliciously. He was too sweet to harm. I'd poke just enough for a laugh but not enough to aggravate him. "Jimmy," I'd say, "I saw you practice kissing with my doll." "No, I did not!" "Oh, really, then why were you in my room yesterday when no one was there?" "I was NOT!"

Jimmy had tantrums. So severe were they that when he held his breath, he'd first turn blue, then purple, until we—my mother, sister, and I—managed to force the breath by cajoling him, pleading with him, yelling at him, and slapping him on the back. His scrunched-up face prevented outside intrusion until that slap on the back or a sudden life force surging up to his reason released him and we all fell into tears as if witnessing a newborn taking its first breath. One day, while my mother was changing his clothes, before she was able to put any clothes on him, he wriggled free, and naked little Jimmy ran out of the house, down the street, until a neighbor caught him and brought him home. That time he was red-faced, crying—maybe looking for his lost father?

After a while, a neighbor across the street befriended our brother. Bud must have been in his thirties or forties, an unmarried adult who treated Jimmy as he would a son, guiding him, mentoring him, serving as a loving role model. Without other kids on the block to play with and without a father, Jimmy spent much of his time across the street with Bud until he entered school and we moved from my grandmother's house to our own.

Over time, Jim harbored resentment toward his absent father. Our father, in his view, ignored his family responsibilities, abandoned his children, and placed his career before his family. When he had children of his own, Jim resolved, he would be that father he'd never had: loving, there for his children, supportive and inclusive. He would be the family man our father never was for us.

My sister was twelve when we arrived in the US, on the cusp of her teenage years. Quiet and shy, reserved and solitary, Vicky, like our mother, kept her deepest feelings to herself. She didn't confide in me, and I dared not intrude. Besides, I was too preoccupied with my own pain. When we entered school in winter 1959, I was sent to the neighborhood grammar school, into the first semester of the sixth grade, as a "midtermer." Vicky entered the second half of the seventh grade at the junior high next door. She delved into her classes, spent her evenings on homework, and received good grades, but did not undertake physical activities. Her heart could not meet the physical challenges. She didn't socialize much but found a good, best friend. Diane, like Vicky, was quiet, a loner, serious, and a close friend and companion to Vicky. I wonder if Vicky and Diane talked intimately, each revealing secrets they would never tell their families. Maybe Diane knew how Vicky felt about coming to this country—about leaving Chile, our father, and our Pisano family. Maybe Diane knew what Vicky thought about her condition being the cause for our move to the US, but neither Vicky nor Diane told me.

So private was my sister that when she, at eighteen years old, decided to go to visit our father and our family in Chile, she didn't tell me, our mother, or our brother why she had made this decision. "I'm going to Chile," Vicky simply told us. Diane, I thought later, must have known why.

There were clues, which I either ignored at the time or was too ignorant to recognize.

My mother makes adjustments to a skirt that Vicky will wear in Chile: Vicky stands in front of the mirror on a table as my mother lets out the hem of Vicky's pleated skirt that she has grown out of and plans to take on her trip. It's now too short and too tight at the waist. My mother tugs down at the skirt that keeps bunching up at Vicky's waist. "Stay still and stop fidgeting!" my mother says through the pins she's holding with her lips. Vicky looks at herself in the mirror, tapping her hands against her tummy, and exclaims, "I've been getting fat lately!"

Neither my mother nor I commented; it would have been offensive to do so.

After Vicky arrived in Chile, my mother received a letter from my father.

"Why didn't you tell me!" I heard my mother's anger as she stormed into my room, letter in hand. "Tell you what?" I answered. "Why didn't you tell me your sister was pregnant!" The shock of this revelation, together with feeling falsely accused of keeping a secret I had no knowledge of, left me numb. I could only remember Vicky looking at herself in the mirror weeks earlier as my mother tugged at Vicky's skirt.

So Vicky was pregnant, and she confided in our father. Had Vicky been afraid to tell us, her now-closest relatives? What consequences was she afraid of? I can only imagine the inner turmoil she must have felt to avoid confrontation and to escape to the world of her lost childhood. There, perhaps, she could find family who would accept her regardless of her situation. At that time, 1965, pregnant unmarried eighteen-year-old girls were shunned or taken to a home for unmarried pregnant girls to give birth and put their babies up for adoption. Vicky avoided the inevitable shame she would face here and take her chances in Chile, albeit a much stricter Catholic country.

Once Vicky's secret was out, my mother contacted Dallis, mother of Greg, the father-to-be. Together they devised a plan. Or, did my mother devise the plan and persuade Dallis to agree to it? Greg was to go to Chile, marry Vicky, and bring her home. He did and brought home a very pregnant Mrs. Rogers. Just to make sure the marriage was recognized in the US, Greg and Vicky married again when they arrived. Soon after, Vicky gave birth to a beautiful baby girl, Cynthia Rogers.

We were a family of secrets, hiding behind our sorrows, afraid to look for comfort in each other. We did, after all, share a life-altering experience. But none of us were able to discuss the impact of that experience on our own personal lives. I didn't confide in my mother. Neither did I confide in my sister. And Jimmy was still too young to have reflected on life experience.

I was too self-absorbed with my own troubles to wonder about theirs, to seek to know and understand the sister hidden behind her external self and to reflect upon the impact that our father's absence would have on my brother. Vicky was kind and protective toward me, and I went no further to explore her psyche. I told her some of my secrets, and she kept them to herself, as she kept her own secrets.

I lacked the language to describe the depths of loneliness I felt and the newfound pleasures I experienced. And I heard no such confidences from my sister. I sensed that both my sister and my brother were similarly absorbed with the demands of their new world, but the unfamiliarity of our surroundings worked to tear apart our previously shared intimacies, as if unfamiliar territory required each of us to find our own way. We loved one another from across a bridge that tied us together but kept us apart. Our shared trait: a turning inward, a closing off, an overt shyness with others, a reluctance to reveal who we really were and where we came from.

Although Jimmy left his—our—past life at only three years old, he too had an empty space where our father had once lived. Too young to know that there could be words for his pain. Too young to understand that he was experiencing feelings of abandonment. Jim attempted to fill the void in myriad ways, some healthy, others less so. A boy who longs for adult male love and companionship and who grows up with three generations of women looks for role models outside the family.

I can't tell my siblings' stories. They would have had to tell their own. I can only tell about them from my point of view, my recollections, and the few photographs I have kept:

The one sister, Vicky, standing straight up, looking at the camera with a soft, tender smile on her five-year-old face. It is a relaxed expression, a somewhat neutral smile: it could be a smile and it could not be a smile. But the smile is in her eyes; they give meaning to what the lower half of her face does not commit to. Her back to the sun, no squinting is needed for her to look at her viewers. Bright sunlight plays with the fine, loose hairs around her head and those long braids—the right one is looped back up and attached to its beginning; the left perhaps hangs down her back but is mostly hidden from view. Short bangs sit this way and that on her forehead. Although she fully presents herself to us, she also hides something. What that is, I don't know and would never learn.

The younger sister, Vivian, is scrunched up, laughing, looking over to the left, tongue between her teeth; you don't want her to laugh too much for fear she'll bite down on that tongue. Her hair is braided too, but her laughing, hunched-up shoulders mask her braids from view. No loose hairs have escaped her braids. Vivian's bangs mostly flow in one direction from a cowlick on the right side of her forehead, and the remaining few bangs turn in the opposite direction. Her eyes squint in merriment; what does she see? Not the photographer, who had no need to tell her to "say cheese," or if he did, she did not hear, being too taken with what she has her mischievous sights on.

The sisters are dressed alike, as if twins: plaid flannel shirts with suspenders. These are clothes their mother sewed. The shirt on the sister with the straight stance, Vicky, remains neatly pressed. Its round collar lies turned down flat, as a collar is intended to lie. The shirt on the scrunched-up sister, Vivian, has been pulled and loosened as if she had been jumping up and down just when the camera stopped time.

I shared a bedroom with my sister for all the time we lived at home. In age, we were barely two years apart. I suppose my mother wanted her girls to be close. She chose names for both of us that started with the same letter: Victoria after her mother-in-law's middle name and Vivian just because it was a *V* name. She dressed us in clothes she constructed from the same pattern, from the same bolt of fabric. People knew Celia's little girls as if they were one: Vicky-and-Vivian. Both wearing plaid shirts and overalls. The one with braids, the other with pigtails. A single room with twin beds, two matching nightstands and two small dressers, and one closet divided in half.

Similarities can make differences stand out. Proximity can cause friction. Sisters who share the same bedroom seek to claim their independence. Vicky had her side of the room and I had mine. During one of our more strenuous arguments, we ran a string right down the center of our room. It was hardly practical. There was no way we could both have access to our one closet and no way for us to divide the entry through the bedroom door. But disputes between Vicky and me never lasted long enough for us to carry out such a plan to a successful conclusion. We each had our own character, demeanor, and friends; and we were tied together by sister love.

In physical appearance, both my sister and I inherited mother's small physique. But unlike my mother and me, my small-statured sister supported breasts that grew into a size-D-cup bra. I believe that her tendency to walk with her size four feet splayed out was not so much an imitation of our beloved grandmother's walk as it was an act of balance. On further reflection, Abuelita also had a large bosom.

In her preteen and teenage years, Vicky had fine, silky light-brown hair cut in a short pageboy style. Hair that so naturally wanted to fall straight, she had to work against its nature to achieve and maintain the pageboy under-curl. That soft curl framed such a delicate face: a heart-shaped mouth, petite nose, brown eyes accented by perfectly arched brows. A face that succumbed to teenage acne but soon evolved into a smooth and creamy texture that stayed with her for the remainder of her life.

I blame that weak heart of hers for setting us off on diverging paths. Ever since we were little, I sought the more physically active, daredevil play. I loved tumbling down a grassy hill, doing handstands and headstands and cartwheels on the lawn. I spent many hours skipping rope with friends, calculating just the right time to jump in, all of us chanting rhymes that moved me to the rope's rhythm.

Vicky's heart condition prevented her from taking part in such physical activities. She tired easily. Running and jumping were not fun. She leaned toward quiescent play.

We both loved the water. In our single-digit ages, we didn't know how to swim, but dressed in our twin yellow Jantzen swimsuits, we could paddle around enough to float, walk in shallow water, and, what we both loved most of all, move hand over hand around the perimeter of the pool. While Vicky rested after the long trek around the pool, I'd skip around on the lawn, causing the half-tutu of my swimsuit to flap up and down. Inner tubes we could not get enough of—sitting on them and propelling backward with windmill backstrokes or lying on our stomachs on top of the tube, paddling forward with alternating strokes.

When Vicky was sick with a cold, I too had to relinquish swimming. We sat together on the lawn next to the pool and watched our cousins splash and do what I so wanted to do too. With me to accompany her, at least Vicky felt better about not being able to swim. I just sulked.

When she did have the energy, Vicky's ventures into sports were not all fun. A fast downhill bike ride at twelve years old resulted in a broken arm. A first ski trip at fifteen lasted only as long as it took her to tumble down the first slope and end up with a compound leg fracture that took months and months to heal. Whether in sympathy for my sister or for fear that I would have the same fate, my mother banned unsupervised skiing for me.

I also had my physical weaknesses, but they were the passing childhood illnesses—measles, mumps, even whooping cough. Every child went through some such afflictions; we didn't have vaccinations for much other than smallpox then. My sister nursed me through those illnesses and then came down with some of them too. Two sick little girls sharing a bedroom, each in her own twin bed.

To me, Vicky was always my big sister and my protector. I felt emboldened to take risks, knowing she would be there to heal my wounds, or help me do something I didn't want to do. After all, I was the little sister. "Go wash your hair, Vivian," my mother would say to me. "But I don't know HOW," I'd whine back. "Vicky, go help your sister." At eleven years old, of course I knew how to wash my own hair. But I liked to have my big sister wash it; to have her soft, pliant fingers gently put my head under a stream of warm, clear water; squeeze beads of honey-rich shampoo on the top of my head; work up a fine white lather; then massage my scalp from forehead to neck and around the ears. So soothing, so luxurious. There was nothing like closing my eyes and leaning back into this pleasure. I decided right then and there never to admit to knowing how to wash my own hair.

Other hands washing my hair would lull me always, even when those hands could no longer be my sister's. Hairdressers would take her place. Even if I'd arrive at the beauty parlor with just-washed hair, I wouldn't deny myself this sensual experience.

Hair—how it looked, how it was managed and cared for—was important to my mother, sister, and me beyond our childhood years. When I was a young child, my mother was our hairdresser. My sister and I had straight hair, as did she. But curls were in. My mother's hairdresser gave her that wavy soft blond look. In those days, having a professional permanent was a typical and nearly all-day affair. Vicky and I experienced the same treatment, but at home. At that age, I didn't care whether or not my hair had curls, hung down straight, or even stuck out every which way. But my mother did. And so she gave us home permanents—about every six months, I think. They were not experiences either of us looked forward to.

My mother first washed my hair—vigorously, not like Vicky's gentle massage. That done, she poured a solution onto my head and rubbed it all around. It had a smell so strong, so pungent, so acrid, I had to hold my breath. Surely it was toxic. Then, starting at the top of my head, she'd section off a small piece of hair. Holding together the ends with a wet square of tissue, she rolled it tightly onto a small pink plastic spool with teeth around it, rolled the spool right up against my scalp, and snapped the lever to close it. That pink contraption was set securely in place and could not jiggle even if I shook my head wildly. This procedure was repeated over and over again until every strand of hair was in its case. Pink rollers sat atop my head as if an extension of my own body. Thirty or fifty of them? My head ached from the strain of the pulled hair.

Before the final step, it was Vicky's turn. I watched my mother do to Vicky what she had done to me, and felt the pulls and scrapes all over again.

To get the best results, my mother poured steaming hot—almost boiling—water over my head, then wound a towel tightly about. With head sensitized by hot water and pressure of the towel, I felt every roller's teeth digging into my scalp. After a sufficient amount of time, the towel was removed for my hair to dry. We didn't have home hair dryers at first, so in those early days the rollers stayed in nearly all day. The hair had to be completely dry before removing the rollers. When we did get dryers—the kind with the shower cap–like bonnet attached with a plastic hose to a portable dryer that you could walk around with (if you had a long-enough extension cord)—I switched the setting to low: my head was still sensitive from the heat it had endured earlier. But then I had to leave the rollers in for a longer time.

I didn't like my permed look. And so successful were the curls that it would be several months before my hair began to relax from its tight, upstart rigid loops.

I loved to watch my mother unwrap Vicky's rollers: her fine hair usually dried before mine, and so I could see the transformation while still awaiting mine. One by one the rollers came off, her hair springing right back up into tight curls, appearing as if it had never been straight at all. My mother gently brushed out the curls to relax the hair's rigidness. But the curls were too stubborn and returned to their tiny tubed positions. I tried not to laugh out loud but could not hold back my laughter, even though I knew what was coming soon. It would be my turn next.

The room that Vicky and I shared in Grandma Stevens's house had an enclosed patio far away from the upstairs bedrooms where my grandmother, mother, and little brother slept, and far away from the downstairs bathroom. Going to the bathroom in the middle of the night required walking across the darkened dining room, opening the swinging kitchen door, fumbling for the light switch, turning right, and walking toward the glass kitchen door. All sorts of fleeting, imaginary faces and noises lurked just outside that door. I needed only to look straight ahead to see that they were there. I'd walk toward them trying not to look through the glass, fearing a confrontation with outdoor demons before finding the door to the tiny bathroom. Luckily, most nights I didn't have to pee. But when I did, I could often count on Vicky to go with me.

The first time Vicky slept over at a friend's house was one of those full-bladder nights. I put off the dreaded walk as long as I could. The night was dark, and I heard noises from the backyard outside our bedroom. Or were they coming from behind the curtain covering the large sliding glass doors? I imagined making the long walk to the toilet. I lay in bed, planning the trip with detailed precision. But each time I mentally rehearsed entering the kitchen, I could not find a way to avoid looking straight at the glass door to the outside. What would be waiting for me there? And if I turned on the light, surely it could see me even if I couldn't see it. Still in my bed, under the warm blankets, I shivered with fear and my dilemma.

I remained there, unmoving, under the covers for as long as I was able to. Then it came, slowly, a warm wet trickle, gathering in momentum as it flowed out about me. *Why isn't Vicky here?*

The next morning, my mother saw sheets and blankets hanging on the clothesline in the backyard. "Vivian, are these yours? What are they doing out here?" As soon as the sun had shown its light that morning, I felt safe enough to get up from the now cold, wet bed and strip the sheets and covers to dry them out on the line. Poor Vicky, my mother forbade her to sleep over at her friend's house again. Did my sister sulk like I did when I was prevented from swimming and skiing? She never told me, and I preferred to bask in her protection rather than think about her privation. I never wet the bed again.

From an early age, Vicky aspired to be a nurse. She imagined herself dressed in a starched white uniform, with white stockings and white, sensible, soft-soled shoes tiptoeing around her patients' beds, her brown hair tucked into a nurse's cap. I picture Nurse Vicky helping others heal, giving aid and comfort to a sick child. For she herself had been a sick child, in the hospital twice for major surgeries before reaching her teens. Her nurses, I imagine, impressed my sister with the ministrations and tender care they gave her. They formed strong role models for a child whose life depended on their protective attention. I imagine the child Vicky in her hospital bed deciding right there and then to follow these ladies in white in their chosen profession. Vicky too would be a nurse like them when she grew up—no doubt about it.

As for me, I was never sure what I wanted to be when I grew up. I didn't want to decide while that future was still so far away. If I did, I'd only be disappointed when it didn't happen the way I'd imagined. Better to have no dream than a dream shattered. No, I'd let my life go where it would.

However, I did share the then-common dream that all girls my age had: marriage in our early twenties. I didn't know or care anything about marriage itself; it was just something taken for granted. But the party was what I looked forward to: The magnificent wedding ceremony. White dress, white flowers, white cake. Bridesmaids in soft pastel colors, the maid of honor striking in a richer, darker hue. Lace and satin and ribbons, sugar-sweet tasty treats, and graceful, swirling dancing would embellish the day. All my girlhood fantasies absorbed from children's books, the church, stories told to children by adults, those same stories elaborated in discussions with friends. Stories ending with "and they lived happily ever after" point to this one, glorious, celebratory day.

In preparation for that day in my own future, I sketched drawings of my wedding dress-to-be: white satin, strapless sweetheart neckline, fitted bodice, a drop-waistline leading to a full floor-length skirt, its long train trailing behind. The white veil held together by a row of white roses atop my brown hair done up in a French twist, just like Grace Kelly's.

That vision would never happen. But my shattered ideal would be no loss by then. I hadn't counted on attaining a changed perspective, replacing conventional dreams with my own. I did not get married in my early twenties, nor any time in my twenties. When I met Paul, I was in my mid-thirties, and though we lived together, we didn't marry until I was forty-two and he fifty-two. We found no need for an elaborate event to commemorate the day. I wore nothing resembling a wedding dress. The simple ritual in the judge's office had no dress code. My weekend pants and shirt served just as well for the vows of allegiance my husband and I made. The judge's secretary served as our witness and photographer. Just four of us comprised our wedding ceremony. I couldn't picture myself in a traditional wedding ceremony: imagining all the pomp, preparations, anxiety, and expense surrounding just such an event tired me. Once the service was over, we were on our way, no rice on our heads and no cans and streamers trailing behind our car. I had outgrown my early fantasy.

My sister never became a nurse. Her life took other turns. Somewhere along the way, she too lost her fantasies; circumstances pulled her out of them. She was a wife, a mother of two, and then a single mother, when she and Greg divorced. Like my mother and grandmother before her, Vicky focused on the immediate situation and what she could do about it. She found employment to support her family and went on to a successful career as a court reporter, her visions of nursing having lost their sparkle even though she had held on to that dream for so long. She never told us how it left her and how its passing affected her.

A Fragile Encounter

Twenty-eight years after our family split apart when we came to the US, my father and his new wife traveled to the US to attend my brother Jim's wedding. We children of estranged parents were filled with anxiety as the wedding date neared. What would this reencounter of our mother and father, ex-husband and ex-wife, be like? And what of our father's current wife? What did she expect? Would our mother be OK?

At the wedding, I watched carefully. My mother wore a pained but masked face as her former husband introduced his wife, Carmen, to her. My heart beat wildly. Did hers, too? Greetings were awkward, yet polite and courteous. Carmen showed a broad, genuine smile. My father's smile looked hopeful. My mother's was strained. Tension tightened my features. All went well throughout the ceremony and reception. My body relaxed. We passed the hurdle. Passions were gone or buried. Champagne was drunk.

Later that evening we gathered at a restaurant for a family dinner. A happy time, celebrating Jim and Ruthie's wedding, our parents with us but not too near each other. I felt the air tinged with electricity and wondered whether others did too. I pretended the tension wasn't there. I'd look to Carmen, the ever-gracious and warm Chilean woman, and avoided my mother's gaze, raw and pained, yet contained. Carmen spoke no English, but she understood, both intrinsically and from her husband's or one of our occasional translations. And she communicated through her radiating smile. My mother, who spoke both languages, said little. Relief and anxiety wrestled within me. I was glad to have Paul by my side. He understood, and that soothed me. My father raised his glass. "A toast to the happy couple, to their life together, to their future family of Pisanos." No translations needed here.

I could see that Jim and Ruthie's elation blinded them to the charged atmosphere. Here we all were, the family unit, together at last.

I worried that feelings repressed over the years could not remain contained. They build, fester, and demand attention. And then came the tipping point, the restaurant bill payment, which my mother and father split. As Paul and I left the restaurant and stepped outside to the parking lot, twenty-eight years of old resentments and pain exploded from my mother.

"You should have paid the entire bill! The least you could do. All those years and you never sent us money!"

"But Celia, I sent what I could. I had little money then, and I couldn't easily send money out of the country."

"You didn't care about us, about your children!"

"Celia, you don't know what I went through."

I saw my mother's wounded expression on view as she vented the grief she had been harboring from the loss and disappointment of her failed marriage. Carmen's smile turned to anguish. My father, too, wore a pained expression. "Your mother," he told me later, "has had a hard life. I feel for her; I didn't want to cause her more pain. I'm sorry if I did." Fortunately, my brother and his new wife were still in the restaurant and did not witness this manifestation of our parents' long-ago love. Vicky and I soothed our mother and led her into the car. The argument was over. There was no sweet making up from that, their final argument.

Dear Vivian

In my early thirties and her early sixties, my mother and I decided to mend cracks in our relationship. We wanted to find a way to reach each other, throwing aside any faultfinding tendencies and petty gripes that pulled us apart. But not, we agreed, with counseling or some other outside help. We hadn't reached that level; we weren't that desperate. Our wish was to repair our relationship with our own will and love for each other. We grieved for a healthier, comfortable bond. Who first came up with the idea to write to each other once a week? It doesn't matter who said it first; it evolved from each of us.

For both of us, writing involved reflection and deliberation, crafting words and phrases carefully to convey intended meaning. No demands of one another, no expectations, no recriminations, just a simple account of what was going on for us during the week. We would write to strengthen the bridge between us.

Years after my mother's death, I collected the letters she had written to me. Not many letters remained, just a shoebox full. Accustomed to moving residences often before I met Paul, I had, by necessity, mastered the art of decluttering. My mother's letters, along with too many other keepsakes, were among its victims.

I devoted an entire summer to transcribing the contents of the shoebox to digital form. I could only proceed slowly. The emotional impact of reading and typing her words was too strong for a fast and uninterrupted pace.

The letters were not, however, deeply emotional. As we had agreed, we'd write about our daily lives, no matter how mundane. Still, her letters touched me deeply fifteen years after her death. They brought her back to me as if she were in the same room, as if she were the one reading her letters. But looking up from the keyboard, scanning the room, I could not see her. She was not there.

Dear Vivian,

Last Tuesday I started to write you a letter as I promised, but I had to change the ribbon. It was so light no one could read it. I could not decipher the system from the directions— it's been so long since I changed it. I struggled about an hour and decided that perhaps the ribbon I brought home from school did not fit. On Saturday I went to Sleepers to buy one specifically for my Remington. I had no more success. Vicky was busy with the wedding of Melisse, so I asked her to come on Sunday and help me. She struggled too, but finally realized what we had been doing wrong. I should have written then, but it was too late since I was going out for bridge and dinner. I am not mechanically oriented, I guess.

Her letters convey a self-deprecating humility, as if to insert a humorous tone. She pokes fun at what she sees as her inadequacies and inexpertness. On this second reading, I'm left with an impression of vulnerability, a woman alone, coping with the complications of everyday life.

Whereas some situations daunt her and leave her beholden to others' help, there are others where she asserts resolute strength and self-assurance. Here she recounts how her teaching methods influenced the students in her high school Spanish class:

Dear Vivian,

My morning classes were delightful. The Spanish 1 class accepted the chastisement of not studying sufficiently for the test. Those who failed or did not receive the grade they expected were eager to study for a make-up test next week. Many A and B grades were made.

And then I recognize an uncompromising harshness toward those who failed to follow her principles:

Period 4 was different. They continued their chatter, looking out the window—it's second lunch period and there is always lots of action in the courtyard—and I felt that those who failed had no intention to study for a make-up. They would take it next week *por si acaso* [just in case] that they might pass. That attitude freezes me. I resent giving up my time to allow them to take the make-up. They will have to learn that attitude means failure.

Farther down this letter, she evokes my sympathy:

Period 5 was a disaster. About halfway through the period, Peter asked me if he could to go the lavatory. I told him it was locked. (We lock the bathrooms because the kids tear them apart or go there to smoke.) He went back to his seat and in about five minutes vomited all over it. I sent my assistant with him to the nurse and ran to the office to call a custodian.

On my return the room was chaos—everyone near the acci-
dent had shuffled the chairs as far away as possible. The class
shouted in unison, "Why don't you call a janitor?" I spread a
bunch of towels I had grabbed in the office on the mess and
screamed: "Why do you think I ran from the room?" Poor
kids, I think they never cleaned up a mess in their young
lives. "You don't know how to react in an emergency except to
scream. That doesn't help anything." They are not intelligent.
I had written out these instructions about the bathroom on a
mimeograph where I described the locking of the restrooms.
If you are sick, ask me for a pass to the nurse. They do not
read instructions. They hate instructions. Well, I guess we all
do. Peter panicked and was embarrassed to tell me. Marike,
our exchange student from Holland, said, "It's dumb to lock
the bathrooms." I told her why—the students go in there
during the periods, tear off the sinks, STUFF TOWELS IN
THE TOILETS, BREAK THE DOOR, and then there are no
restrooms for several weeks. She was appalled. "In Europe we
do crazy things, graffiti on the walls, but it would never occur
to us to engage in that kind of vandalism."

I don't have any of my letters to her. Perhaps she kept them in an old
shoebox that was tossed after her death. I can only infer from reading my mother's letters what I had written in mine. I seem to have
conveyed to her the image of a woman looking to establish herself,
contemplating quandaries and turning to her mother seeking reassurance. In her letters, I received motherly, encouraging advice:

Dear Vivian,
   Decisions! Vivian, don't worry about them; you only get
high blood pressure. Do the best you can and live with it. I
found that to be very true. As Pangloss says, "This is the best

of all possible worlds." There is no going back—only forward. I think you made the choice that you wanted—make the most of it. If you are dissatisfied, you can always back up and go another way. You are young. I may always feel sad about not taking the job in San Diego, but I made that decision to stay here. I am satisfied now, and though I may have not made the best decision, I do not know how it would have turned out, and I am safe and secure in Sacramento with a good position. Perhaps old age reaches for security while youth would rather take chances.

This letter ends on a note that melts my heart:

> I can go on writing forever, but I am sure you are tired of my rambling. Receiving your letter is a great joy. I hope mine creates the same feeling in you.
>
> All my love, my darling Vivian,
> Mommy

I don't know how long we kept our letter-writing routine. The last letter I have is from 1987, over thirty years ago. I know our written exchanges wound down and eventually stopped without either of us making a conscious decision to do so. I like to think we reached an unspoken understanding: we've made a connection—our relationship may continue to be rocky, but rocky on solid ground.

My mother knew how to hide what she didn't want her children to know. Are there secrets she kept from me that she might have told me some evening, late into our lives when we had finally reached level ground? Mother and daughter reminiscing, reconciling, admitting and accepting each other's mistakes and flaws. "Remember the time when . . . ?" "I just wanted to protect you from . . ." "I didn't know you felt that way, else I wouldn't have . . ."

"Never mind now, we understand each other, and any old barriers between us are dissolved."

We never got there. If her intent was there, the means to communicate was lost to the stroke she suffered during the last couple of years of her life. If, at an earlier time, my desire to share revelatory moments with my mother had broken through, I cannot be sure I would have had the maturity to receive her deepest thoughts without bungling the message, unable to see through my own faults to accept my mother's. I had no tools then to help me work through slipups in a bond that had been sewn together so long ago.

In her house I learned to live within the role parameters that my mother defined for her family: mother knows best, child adapts; mother provides, child benefits; mother shields child from adult hardships, child focuses on her own troubles.

What I unearth today looks different from how I experienced it at the time. I have changed. I am older. Time has shorn away resentments. The tension I felt then has dissolved. I am shaped by two cultures, one I was born into and another that adopted me. My first experiences in this adopted country led me to resist an easy transition and to nurture an idealistic picture of the native country I had left behind. My resistance was my proclivity until it melted away. My resentments toward my mother followed, although they left me too slowly.

Now I think about my mother with a lighter, gentler touch, as if her death has caused a certain bitterness in me to die. The perspective of my youthful self has been replaced by one formed over the course my life has taken. What felt real to me then seems less so now; those past experiences carry less weight, and frankly I've largely forgotten their impact. I now look at the memories and that relationship with a new perspective. Gone is the irritation I had felt trying to make her see me for who I was and not what I thought she thought I should be. Gone too is my desire to have seen her as I would've liked her to be.

On the wall calendar hanging in my mother's kitchen, Tatiana had written the only entry for 1995, the first day of spring, March 21: *Celia died. 11:15 a.m. (oh dear!)*. Tatiana, the live-in caretaker my sister hired for my mother's last year, had grown close to her. Tatiana looked after my mother in a way that neither I, nor my sister or brother, could have done. My mother's stroke the year and a half before had left her in a wheelchair, unable to speak and too weak to swallow. She lived with a feeding tube for a large part of the time following her stroke.

I stood at the entrance of the funeral home's viewing room, a large space opened for the immediate family, prior to funeral services for the public. It was eerily empty. The floor was covered with wall-to-wall industrial-looking carpet made from some durable stain-resistant fiber, likely to absorb sounds of wailing. Minimize the survivors' disturbance.

A sprinkling of sympathy flowers, floral sprays, and memorial wreaths provided some color in the empty, gray space. On a dais at the far side sat the casket that Vicky and I had selected—a simple traditional style with pink taffeta lining. From where I stood at the doorway, I could see a head resting on a puffy pink pillow. Vicky had insisted on an open casket. I relented after a feeble protest. And just then, I wished I had been a stronger advocate. In that same moment I saw the absurdity of our color selection. The only pinks I saw my mother wear were the bold and shocking pinks of her Vera scarf or her dress with large, bright pink blobs partnered with tangerine orange circles. Pale, lacy pinks were not in her fashion vocabulary.

I walked on shaky legs toward the casket, thankful to have a carpet below me. The mortician intended family and friends to pay their last respects to a loved one as if they were alive, just merely in a peaceful sleep. I looked into the casket at my mother's body. It was her but not her. A painted rubber doll that I could not touch, much less kiss as my sister had just done.

Fragments of tender moments, old arguments, and images of my mother in life flashed before me while I stared inside the silent casket. A carousel of memories marched one after another in no particular order:

We, mother and daughter, look at our images together in the mirror, pleased by the bond and similarities we see in our reflection.

My mother, barely able to hold back uncharacteristic tears, turns to me, her obstinate daughter: "Why are you always so critical of me?!"

My American mother in Chile, out in our front yard, wearing shorts when no other woman would be seen wearing anything other than a below-the-knees skirt.

A ten-year-old me, sitting on my father's lap, answers, "Only for a visit," when he asks me if I'd like to go to the US. "Celia," he shouts to my mother in the other room, "did you hear what Vivian said?" I hear a muffled "Yes," and I feel a premonition.

My closet sanctuary where I, alone in the dark, whisper questions I could never ask her, "Can we go back home, to Chile? I don't like it here."

My mother, the self-sufficient, hard-driving, tearless, demanding single mother in a rare personal moment of disclosure turns to me to answer my question, "Mom, why didn't you ever remarry?" "Because I still love your father."

My mother, playing bridge with her friends as she proudly introduces me.

My mother, dressing my sister and me in twin outfits fresh from her sewing machine.

My mother, drunk, swaying the car side to side as she negotiates the curves on Highway 1. I look down the cliffs to the breaking waves far down below.

My mother's words, unspoken yet written there, in her letters to me: "I'm here, with you, my darling Vivian." "Merry Christmas, my dear Vivian." "All my love, Mommy."

My mother, the conflicted, complicated, closed, close, comforting presence.

My mother. I turned away from the lifeless casket. There I saw Vicky and Jim. I thought about how my mother and our family life had shaped our lives. What if we had never left Chile—what would this moment mean to each of us? And those whose presence and absence had such significance to who I am today: how would their influence have changed, had our circumstances been different? I mourned my father six thousand miles away, my two culturally distant and now long-gone grandmothers, my large and ever-growing Chilean family.

I reminded myself, I am here today for my mother, who took us by her side and nurtured us in the way she knew how throughout her life. And I wished I could have shown gratitude for what she gave me rather than blaming her for what was taken away from me. Yet I could find no words for that rubber image. Whimpering sounds reached me from behind. Tatiana, my mother's devoted caretaker, was softly crying.

I am left with the questions I could not ask her when she was alive. There's no one to ask. And so, I look for answers and clues. I poke at my own memories, even as they fade with every advancing year. I take them as they emerge—write them down and work them over as one rolls around a lemon on the counter with gentle pressure to allow its juices to flow upon puncturing it. Sometimes a seed encapsulating a long-ago scene spews out.

I drift in and out of sleep, with a sheet covering my heated body, red blotches all over my body and on my swollen face. It's the middle of the day, the sunlight kept out of the room by the heavy cotton drapes. The darkness soothes my eyes. I have little energy for any activity, so I pass the time looking at the patterned olive-green drapes, counting the tulip blossoms arranged in vertical rows. Sounds of kids playing just outside the opened windows seem far away; I wonder if the measles has spread to my ears or the drapes serve to muffle noises. I'm too tired to figure it out. I kick the sheet off my burning-hot body, reach for the mirror on my nightstand, bring it up to my face. I hardly recognize my seven-year-old self. Instead I see an alien and imagine living my life in isolation, too different to join in the company of others.

Dear Mom

Dear Mom,

I regret.

I regret not understanding and not forgiving you. As soon as we arrived here, to your home country, I wanted to go back to mine. *"Yo quiero ir a Chile,"* I wrote in tiny handwriting inside the walk-in closet that Vicky and I shared at Grandma Stevens's house in Sacramento. So small and hidden that you couldn't see it, but there, in writing, in case you would. I couldn't speak to you what was in my heart. I expected you to know. I expected you would know through my attitude and appearance. And, I was afraid of what your answer might be.

I regret not telling you how I felt.

Throughout my teens, I thought of you as the person who wouldn't acknowledge my sorrow, pushed me in directions you chose, and held me back from what I wanted to do, where I wanted to go. I didn't even know what or where that was, but I was too proud to seek guidance.

I regret blaming you.

I blamed you for ripping me away from Chile and bringing us to this foreign country that claimed the name America, in spite of all the other American countries in the Western Hemisphere. I had felt contempt from the few Americans I'd known in Chile. They seem to flaunt their America over ours, an undeveloped country. I did not want to live among such arrogance.

You separated me from my world; I needed to separate from you.

I regret my youthful contemptuous attitude.

I regret doing wild and crazy things. And I regret my hurt and my shame when you called me on something wild and crazy that I did and shouldn't have done.

I regret not being the dutiful daughter I wish I could have been.

I regret not understanding how much you loved me and your pride in me. I only heard from others, years later, "Your mother was so proud of you, your education, your career." Those things you wanted me to achieve, I achieved. Those things you had always wanted for me, I got. Those things you revered—education, literature, study, work—I did those things, in spite of my rebelliousness and my staunch stubbornness not to emulate you, not to do those things you wanted me to do. I'm like you.

And I don't regret it.

As with many of my youthful ways, I lost my propensity for boredom. Not by doing things I didn't want to do, but by creating choices for myself, looking for delights in the disagreeable, and using that time for self-reflection and discovery. And, admittedly, my mother's underlying message of "Get to work!" did reach me. I did get to work, took it seriously, found satisfaction in working, and, if less than satisfactory, found ways to make it interesting. If that failed, I learned to leave gracefully and reach for something else. Today, as I look out my window, I find a subdued, softly shining, melancholy fall morning. Yellows, deep maroon reds, and browns of all varieties litter the ground: detritus from yesterday's moderate winds and rain. Dark but shallow pools of water pattern the driveway. Images outside my window stir my insides and poke at memories.

Toward the end of my mother's life, as she became increasingly debilitated by physical ailments and illnesses, I struggled to feel sympathy. I should, I can't, I'll try, I fail. My sister, on the other hand, provided care and attention, genuinely and consistently. One could say that it was easier for her, as she lived only a few blocks away, whereas I lived a hundred miles away. But still, I do not forgive myself so easily.

On one of those days, I resolved to be a better daughter, to not let my own bitterness overtake genuine affection. I would be taking my mom for a Sunday dinner at a favorite restaurant of hers next to the Sacramento River.

I arrived at her house in the late afternoon. She was dressed nicely, her makeup and perfume overdone for my taste, but I kept that to myself. Slowly I helped her get in the car. It was a beautiful fall day for a drive alongside the river. The air was bright and crisp, and the landscape was filled with orange, red, yellow, and variegated leaves hanging on and draping maple trees. Smells of damp, rich earth floated by in the light breeze. As we neared the river, weeping willows and other deciduous trees and plants converted the landscape into colorful greens.

We found a parking space right in front of the restaurant. But it was still a long, slow walk to the entrance, my mother holding on to me on one side and to her new, stylishly graceful cane on her other side. The restaurant had a pleasant atmosphere, as if it were a large dining room in an elegant house. We were seated to the side of the room, with plenty of maneuvering space and views of the coming sunset out the windows.

There was nothing in particular—it never is any one thing in particular—but old resentments started stirring inside me. Critical, judgmental was what I felt. But I was determined not to violate my resolve. As we ate our meal, I could see some discomfort in my mother's face.

I then recalled another, earlier outing, a weekend for just the two of us at the Benbow Inn in Northern California. Immediately after dinner on our second evening, we returned to our room. Tension had ruled the meal. We sat across from each other at the table, but we said few words. I could hardly glance up from my meal to look at her. I was tired of her drinking and more so of its being a taboo subject. It caused me to be distant, uncommunicative, and bitter. It gave rise to that other subject we could never discuss: the breakup of our family, the separation from my homeland and all we had left behind in Chile—my father, my beloved abuelita, my extended family, and my happy childhood. I never felt allowed to discuss the circumstances with her or to acknowledge the loss.

As my mother pulled down the covers and climbed in her bed, she erupted, "Why are you always so critical of me?!" Violently she turned to face the wall and said nothing more.

I wondered, as I sat across from her in that Sacramento River road restaurant: Does bitterness show on my face?

I noticed a man seated at a nearby table who had been looking our way, and at me, throughout the evening. Perhaps he sensed my turmoil; perhaps he saw and resented my callousness. His gaze felt like a cold, hard stare.

Time to go. While helping my mother stand, I saw liquid running down her leg, pooling at her feet, on the carpet below. Not a word from her; was she pretending it was not happening? I got up, walked across the room, and apprised the waitress. As I passed his table on the way back, the man whose unnerving look had shamed me stopped me.

"You are a very faithful and caring daughter attending to your dear mother. I've watched how you minister to her, and I applaud you for taking her on an outing, to this restaurant. It is not easy living with illness, being cooped up; I can see you truly cherish your mother. Thank you for being there for her in her time of need."

There was nothing to say; I could find no words to correct him. I didn't deserve this praise. It was my sister, not me, who was the caretaker. I was the errant daughter whose guilt was now compounded by an onlooker's misguided praise.

I went back to the table, helped her up, and this time felt resentments washed away by this man's earnest words, leaving a pure sense of mother-daughter connection. I walked with my mother, mom, mommy across the floor, a dark stain on the back of her dress for all to see. And, on the carpet, her own patterned pool. We walked out into the now-darkened outside, all the fall colors joining together, resting.

EPILOGUE

On my dresser sits an oblong hand-painted dish from Grandma Stevens. It comes from a set of hand-painted dishes she inherited from her mother and is one of several passed on to me. Every piece has its own unique design. On this thirteen-inch tray, a delicate hand scattered pastel pink roses with pale yellow centers embedded in green foliage that followed the elongated shape of the dish. Two gilded lines run around the base, as does another line marking its perimeter. Golden decorative handles frame each end of the oblong dish.

What was its intended use—as a tray for olives? Cheese and crackers? No, this dish is too dainty for savory hors d'oeuvres. I can imagine only fancy candies and little decorated cakes on this tray. It's suited for small tea parties. For ladies with graceful fingers picking up small, sweet morsels they can keep in their mouth in between sips of dark tea. I picture my grandmother hosting not a ladies' tea on a warm spring afternoon, but an evening women's bridge game.

Parties are no longer its purpose, now that it is mine. This ceramic dish, besides eliciting mental wanderings about my long-gone grandmother, serves as a kind of catch-all tray. Here go small artifacts that I want close to me for practical or aesthetic or sentimental reasons. To wit: Two pairs of tiny scissors, one for clipping fine edges of fingernails that my blunt-cutting nail clipper cannot manage, the other for clipping plastic tags from new clothing. Safety pins of various sizes, for those occasions when I don't want to bother taking the time to retrieve one from my stash in the next room, as well as safety pins I've removed from tags of clothing and put there when I don't want to take the trouble to go to the next room just to store one tiny safety pin where it belongs.

Items that have no other home belong here too. Where else would I put a half-inch star tile that a tile worker in Morocco carved for me after I expressed admiration for his work? And a tiny basket—its handle broken off—woven by a craftswoman from my brother-in-law's caning shop?

The most cherished objects in my ceramic tray are like the tray itself: traces of lost family, mementos that tie me to departed loved ones. Here lives an inch-wide, silver-plated filigree perfume vial from my abuelita. I open the screw top mounted with a tiny turquoise stone, lift the glass applicator to my nose, and take in its scent, even though the vial has held no liquid perfume for over fifty years. And for me in that moment, Abuelita comes alive.

A two-inch round mirror, its back side ornamented silver and at its center, my initials inscribed in antique cursive, was a gift from my sister, gone now for over ten years. The silver needs polishing, as does the perfume vial. But I leave them as they are and as they wish to age. I lift up the tarnished mirror to my face. What do I have in common with my sister's visage? The nose, although hers was more delicate, smaller than mine. Eyebrows? No. Hers were nicely shaped and plucked—especially those stray hairs that bridged them. She tamed the eyebrows she inherited from our father. And mine? They're like my mother's, nonexistent as they taper out. Yet there's familiarity in the eyes, in the manner they communicate. Father, mother, grandmother, sister, brother—traces of them all are in that mirror. But surely I see a more wrinkled face than ever was my sister's. I am now ten years older than she when she died.

From my father, a Bausch & Lomb triplet magnifier. An appropriate tool for a botanist's pocket. I can use it to inspect the detailing in the decoration of his mother's perfume vial or the flowers painted on his mother-in-law's dish. Or, I can take it outside to the garden, where through its lenses even the most uninvited, unappealing weed shows beauty.

Tokens of people close to me are sprinkled throughout my house. But it is here, on my dresser, in my ceramic tray that daily I encounter the nearness of those who are gone.

Neither my mother nor my brother is represented here. My brother? His death is still too fresh, too recent. I don't need reminders. He still dwells in my daily thoughts. And my mother? For now, writing this account of remembrances of her keeps us attached.

Writing this memoir has been transformative. I no longer feel I'm the difficult daughter I was when my mother was alive. But what good does that do? you may ask. Exactly—it may do no one any good or make any difference. Except for me. It relieves me. It makes me wish I could speak to her through the wall between life and death: "Mommy, I love you." Curiously, guilt doesn't intervene. I'm past that stage. Too late—I'm too old to acquire newly found guilt. I can only take the peace of mind this process has given me.

I wonder, too, what late thoughts she had in life, about me, my siblings, her long-lost husband. Did she come to a peace of mind? A resolution? Love? I can only hope so. She delivered a message to me last night in a dream.

I'm in a large house, as if designed by Julia Morgan, hexagonal, wood interior, open beamed ceiling. I need to go to the bathroom. I go and do my business. But I can't leave my waste material there. I have to get rid of it somewhere else. Where? I don't know. I pick it up, try to stuff it in a plastic bottle I have. It fits. Where to trash it?

I walk out into a large hall, look around. A trash can: I throw my container away. I turn around to look at the hall. There I see my mother, walking toward me slowly. She looks youngish, as if in her fifties or maybe sixties. Blond hair as always. But on the lower part

*of her face I notice a red-purple color. Blood has drained and pooled
there. She is dead, I know. "Mommy," I say. I'm overwhelmed with
tenderness—mine and what I can see of hers, in her eyes. "Mommy,"
and I go to hug her.*

I woke up with the knowledge that I have come to terms with
my love for my mother. Any vileness between us is gone. I have dis-
carded it and am left with understanding and loving appreciation.

I have gone back to Chile several times, acknowledging my roots
there but stepping lightly. I've made a good life here in my adopted
country: loving husband, comfortable home, long and satisfying
career. And yet when asked to choose between my two identities, I
wonder if by choosing one I'm rejecting the other. Does belonging
have only one place? I'm still asking myself. I still don't know.

Belonging feels foreign to me. Can I know who I am without
knowing where I belong? Am I Hispanic or non-Hispanic? I'm torn
when faced with choosing between these two options that appear
on the census form and increasingly on other forms and applica-
tions. If I check one category, next time I'll check the other. I'm not
sure if the question is one of self-identity or of genetic identity. And
what if the Hispanic side of the family—my father's side—identifies
itself more with its European roots rather than its Indigenous ones?
I have a foot in two worlds, but no place to embed either one.

Vivian and Vicky, in two worlds—Sacramento (above) Limache (below).

Celia Stevens Pisano (above) Grandma Stevens (below)

The Pisanos (above) Edmundo and Raul (below)

Celia and Vicky

Vivian

Jimmy

Three siblings

Young Celia in Limache (above) Two sisters dressed alike (below)

Crocker Elementary Sixth Grade class with Vivian (front center) and Sue (second row, second from right)

Cousin Eugenia and Vicky

Best friends at St. Margaret's

Jim, Raul, and Sylvia

ACKNOWLEDGMENTS

This book is the result of many who have showed me to light the writing spark, mold and shape it into a story, guided me through one revision after another, and nurtured and encouraged me to keep writing, keep crafting,

Thank you to my instructors:

Susan McCombs, my first Creative Non-Fiction instructor, had me writing personal essays week after week for several years, repeatedly encouraging me to dig deeper. Susan, I give you credit for suggesting and helping me organize my patchwork of essays into one cohesive whole.

Deborah Lichtman, whose sharply focused writing classes introduced me to tools and techniques for writing and crafting memoir.

David Schweidel, Linda Joy Meyers, Tamim Ansary, and Brooke Warner are instructors and coaches who have shared their expertise and constructive critique in classes and workshops I have taken over the years.

I will end this section to begin at the beginning: To Katherine Young who, in her Fall 2011 OLLI (Osher Lifelong Learning Institute) class, "Philosophy of the Senses," extolled my writing and encouraged me to take a writing path: Thank you; I would not have thought to open a door I had not seen before.

Thank you to readers of my manuscript:

Martina Reaves, Anna Rabkin, Nancy MacKay, Caroline Purves, Jan Camp, David Guthartz, Sandra Strothers, Leslie Rodd, Joanne

Cooke, Sue Botelho, Adrianne Aron. Your comments and suggestions have enhanced and given shape to this work.

A heartfelt thanks to members of my writing groups who have given me feedback on excerpts of my memoir:

Addison Street Writers Circle—Sue Ezekiel, Karen Grassle, Ruth Hanham, Eleanor Lew, Kate Pope, Anna Rabkin, Martina Reaves, Maryly Snow, Linda Sondheimer.

FAB Memoir Group—Adrianne Aron, Jacque Ensign, Elizabeth Hutchins, Susan Kurjiaka, Martha Luehrmann, Georgie Ziff.

Each of you has left your mark on these pages.

Thank you for the book's design and editing:

Jan Camp, I am so thankful for your graceful hand leading me through the publishing process. Your encouragement of a reluctant author, your expertise in book design and formatting, and the myriad of book production activities. I couldn't have come this far without you.

For your keen copyediting mind and sharp proofreading eyes, Elissa Rabellino, I am so grateful.

And for the cover artwork, as well as inspiration and support:

Paul Widess, my partner in life, thank you for an insightful rendition of my story and for being here with me.

ABOUT THE AUTHOR

Vivian Pisano has been writing personal essays, memoir and short fiction since 2010, when she retired from a long career in librarianship. Her work has won awards and recognition, and some of her stories and memoir pieces have been published in journals and anthologies. Vivian lives in Berkeley, California with her husband.

CPSIA information can be obtained
at www.ICGtesting.com
Printed in the USA
LVHW041350120322
713311LV00005B/264